I0796429

Praise for *Lead Solo*

"*Lead Solo* is entertaining, educational, and motivational. Frank brings the reader into the cockpit during the Blue Angel flight training and airshow performance. The values, life lessons, and experiences will be carried long past the exhilaration of flight. This is a great read." **—Connie Bowlin, Delta Airlines' fourth female pilot, president of EAA Warbirds of America, and Honorary Ace & Georgia Aviation Hall of Fame recipient**

"Whether you are in the back seat, on his wing, or reading this book you will experience the values Cdr. Frank Weisser has demanded of himself and is now sharing with us. He takes you with him through adversity and failure, showing the importance of high standards of character. No matter what our own endeavor might be, Commander Weisser challenges us to be the best. Next time, you will watch the Blue Angel demonstration with a new appreciation." **—Bob Hoff, CEO of Aero Mark and FAA's Wright Brothers Master Pilot Award Recipient**

"Have you ever feared failure? Do you want to be inspired? Interested in a behind-the-scenes glimpse of what it takes to be a Blue Angels pilot? If you answered yes to any of these questions, this book is for you!" **—Brian Terwilliger, film producer and director of *Living in the Age of Airplanes* and *One Six Right***

"As a former Blue Angels pilot and a key contributor to the blockbuster movie *Top Gun: Maverick*, Weisser shares how his unique flying experiences shaped his perspectives on trust, communication, adversity, and courage. His insights go beyond the cockpit, offering readers valuable lessons on leadership and resilience in both the sky and everyday life." **—@combat_learjet**

LEAD SOLO

Learning Life's Vectors from an F/A-18 Blue Angel Aviator

CDR. FRANK WEISSER, USN (RET.)

Naval Institute Press
Annapolis, Maryland

Naval Institute Press
291 Wood Road
Annapolis, MD 21402

ISBN: 978-1-68247-666-6 (Hardcover)
ISBN: 978-1-68247-667-3 (eBook)

Library of Congress Cataloging-in-Publication Data is available.

♾ Print editions meet the requirements of ANSI/NISO z39.48-1992 (Permanence of Paper).
Printed in the United States of America.

33 32 31 30 29 28 27 26 25 9 8 7 6 5 4 3 2 1
First printing

CONTENTS

PREFACE

THIS IS NOT A MEMOIR. This is not my story. In fact, before I could even make the claim of being worthy of a book or memoir, I could quickly name a dozen people with whom I've served—mentors, teammates, wingmen, peers, and subordinates—who are far more deserving of such a honor.

This book is intended to be a short illustration of the lessons I've learned while serving alongside them and flying on their wing. In these pages, I attempt to share some of those experiences and the ideas I've taken from them with those who haven't had the privilege of serving with so many great Americans. I am profoundly grateful for having had the opportunity, and I feel strongly that it is my responsibility to share their stories and their greatness.

There is no doubt that my naval career had two facets that seem to get the most attention: flying with the Blue Angels and flying in *Top Gun: Maverick*. They are certainly what elicit the most interest and questions. Despite that, neither of those two aspects of my career come anywhere close to the top of my list, nor are they what I am most proud of. They were helpful in learning and illustrating some of the themes I will discuss herein, but they were not the foundation of my career, nor were they the exclamation point.

I am unquestionably most proud of my combat deployments and my time spent patrolling the skies over Iraq and Afghanistan in a supporting role to the brave Americans, our men and women, on the ground there. Those days and nights are undeniably what I hold most dear and supply my most vivid memories of my time in the service of our great nation. I am also grateful for the relationships forged at sea and ashore, the relationships that provide the true meaning in my life. So many of us came into aviation, especially military aviation, with a desire to fly these incredible machines. But I believe I'm not alone in having my experiences in the aircraft be a distant second to the time spent with the exceptional men and women I served alongside that left me better for the journey.

When I'm invited to speak to groups, large or small, I share cockpit footage from Blue Angels air shows and behind the scenes videos from *Top Gun: Maverick*; but the highlight is always a video of a night carrier landing. It reminds me each time that what often generates the most attention can be essentially a distraction from the real subject. As I write this and even as you read this, our brave brothers and sisters are serving on one of the most dangerous environments in the world: the flight deck of a carrier while others launch off the front end into the darkness. All this is done to support our deployed forces, in harm's way, serving us day and night. For all of them, I am eternally grateful.

My hope is that this book might in some small way inspire or motivate you, perhaps in the same way the Blue Angels attempt to motivate and inspire as they travel around the world, showcasing the pride and professionalism of the

United States Navy and Marine Corps. It is never too early to effect positive change in your life, and it is never too late to reinvent yourself for the better.

> ***"The best time to plant a tree was twenty years ago. The second best time is now."***
>
> ***—ANONYMOUS PROVERB***

CHAPTER 1

FOCUS

"The successful warrior is the average man, with laser-like focus."

—BRUCE LEE

"SOLOS, WE'RE CLEARED for takeoff—maneuver: our section takeoff maneuvers. Let's run 'em up!" That ten-second radio call began the aerial portion of the Blue Angel air show demonstration for me, as the Lead Solo pilot, and my wingman, the Opposing Solo pilot.

We each advanced our throttles to 80 percent, confirmed the engines and afterburner nozzles were programmed properly, ensured all other displays and gauges were in the normal and expected ranges, and then looked inward of our formation at each other's jets to ensure our configurations were correct. Most important for me, I checked that my wingman had his flaps at the "Half" setting, which was the traditional flap setting for takeoff in an F/A-18, and even more important, he verified that my flaps were in the "Up" position. That small little detail, if overlooked, could have meant the almost immediate loss of aircraft and life shortly after rotation for the Lead Solo's takeoff maneuver, the Dirty Roll. Any position other than full Up so significantly reduces the roll rate that the jet would not have been able to complete the 360-degree roll before impacting the runway from which it just lifted off. Mistakes as a pilot, even a Blue Angels pilot, are expected—it certainly isn't a zero-defect organization. But that particular mistake, overlooking that specific detail of the flap setting, is irrevocable, which is why we had "two-person integrity" to prevent the possibility of a single point of failure and a subsequent catastrophic mistake.

So the *easy* part is done, and it's time to go to work.

"Off brakes: Now. Blowers ready: Now!" And with that even shorter radio call, we both release our brakes on the first "now" and move the throttles forward to full afterburner on the second "now." The cadence and timing of this maneuver, like all Blue Angel maneuvers, are absolutely critical. To execute this correctly, it's not just that both pilots must move their throttles at the same time; rather, they must move them at the same time, with the same speed, and at the same rate of change. Anything other than that puts them out of position instantly. These small details, while likely impossible to notice to the untrained eye, are what make the Blue Angels an internationally known Demonstration Team.

Off roar two U.S. Navy Blue Angel F/A-18 Hornets, both accelerating under the power of 32,000 pounds of thrust, making them almost exactly a 1:1 thrust-to-weight ratio on takeoff. Traditionally, when Navy jets depart from a runway, even as part of a two-plane section or four-plane division, each pilot waits ten to fifteen seconds after the previous jet has taken off. Less traditional is a section takeoff where both planes release brakes together and execute their takeoff roll at the exact same time. When this occurs, the wingman is typically aft on an approximate 30–45 degree bearing line, each splitting their half of the runway to ensure no wingtip overlap should the lead jet have to abort for any reason. People don't attend air shows to see the ordinary, so the Blue Angels find ways to make even something as benign as a takeoff more exciting.

This maneuver is performed abeam one another, meaning perfectly in line going down the runway. This makes the physical ergonomics of the pilot "flying" formation, despite still being on the runway, that much harder because they are having to look across their body rather than comfortably forward. Checkpoints are also harder to line up when pilots are abeam one another, further adding to the complexity of this takeoff maneuver. The Lead Solo pilot normally takes off on the left side of this formation, and the Opposing Solo pilot is on runway centerline. On a normal runway with a width of 150 feet, if the Lead Solo has his left main landing gear only 5–10 feet from the edge of the paved runway and they each have a wingspan of 45 feet, then the wingtips are approximately only 10 feet apart as these two jets rapidly accelerate down the runway.

At 170 knots (nautical miles per hour), which is roughly 195 mph (only 5 knots less than the absolute max speed for the nose landing gear), the Lead Solo aggressively rotates the jet to a 30-degree, nose-up climb while simultaneously deselecting afterburner. When done properly, the Lead Solo can achieve that 30-degree climb angle almost before the main landing gear lift off, providing a dynamic picture of the two jets side by side, with the outboard (further away from the crowd) jet still level and on the runway and the inboard jet essentially established in the climb. Despite always wanting excess power, the afterburners are deselected to allow the crowd to see the billowy white smoke trailing the jet—leaving the engines in afterburner causes the exhaust air to be so incredibly hot that the smoke is burned and rendered invisible. Mere seconds later, at the lowest altitude that the maneuver can be safely executed, the Lead Solo pilot rolls the jet 360 degrees while leaving the landing gear down, complicating the maneuver because the drag caused by the gear significantly undermines the jet's acceleration and performance. All this just to demonstrate what an incredibly powerful and dynamic aircraft the U.S. Navy has the privilege to fly!

While all that is occurring, one of the most critical points in the Blue Angels' forty-five-minute demonstration is taking place just a few feet away. The Opposing Solo pilot has pulled back ever so slightly on the stick with his right hand, providing just enough force to cause the jet to lift off the ground, while simultaneously moving the landing gear handle to the up position with his left hand. The landing gear is intelligently designed so that it cannot be raised without "Weight Off Wheels" (WoW), but the intent of this maneuver is to seemingly stay at taxi height despite being airborne with both a gear and flap transition occurring while the jet accelerates from 170 knots to over 300 knots in just a few thousand feet of remaining runway.

Almost as if runways were specifically designed for Blue Angel air shows, the Opposing Solo pilot flying in the #6 jet reaches his ideal high-performance-climb maneuvering airspeed at the same point the runway ends. This is quite a benefit as runways typically have trees or roads or a variety of other obstructions on either or both the arrival or departure ends, and a jet at that low of an altitude would certainly have to alter the maneuver to execute it safely. Once the vertical speed is reached, the Opposing Solo pilot puts both hands on the stick, allowing for more precise control, and pulls back, demonstrating the dramatic climb rate and angle of the Hornet and subjecting his body to six or seven times the force of gravity.

Blue Angel F/A-18s, while having spent the majority of their "lives" flying off aircraft carriers in various Navy fighter squadrons, undergo a few key modifications prior to becoming air show jets. The paint scheme is the most obvious of all—it has stood the test of time, and our airplanes today look almost identical to how they looked in 1946 when the first Blue Angel team took to the sky. We also remove the 20 mm Vulcan canon from the nose of the jet. We certainly don't need that incredibly powerful and precise gun, which can destroy a vehicle with a single round, while we're flying air shows. Instead, in that same location we install a tank that allows us to carry the smoke oil that turns into that beautiful white smoke once it enters the jet's exhaust. One final, and not well-known, Blue Angel modification is the installation of a spring that the engineers call the AFS, or Artificial Feel Spring. We can vary the tension on the spring mechanically, but the entire air show season is flown with the spring simulating approximately forty pounds of force, essentially pulling the stick forward. So, in effect, it takes a forty-pound bicep curl with your right hand and arm to maintain level flight and a great deal more force to effect a climb or level high-G turn.

I'm sure you are asking why in the world the Blue Angels would want to add something that causes the jet to nose over with forty pounds of pressure when unattended, or why they would want to physically exhaust themselves with that level of seemingly unnecessary exertion over the course of the entire air show (the spring doesn't come off ever during the show), so I'll explain. Even though the F/A-18 is an incredibly high-performance jet, and even though it has a fly-by-wire flight control system, there still remains a small amount of ambiguity: a "dead zone" or a "null zone" where you can move the stick ever so slightly and the jet doesn't move accordingly. Because of the incredibly close formations and low-altitude maneuvers made during the show, the pilots require total control and must eliminate that null zone, and thus the spring was born and is one of the great secrets of our show.

With all that now said, back to Blue Angel #6, the Opposing Solo pilot. As he accelerates down the runway, with the jet off the ground, the landing gear raised, and maintaining a mere foot above the runway, he experiences something most analogous to having a rocket ship strapped to his back. If at any time during that takeoff maneuver he were to relax that forty-pound curl by even an eighth of an ounce, the jet would crash in less than a second. To do that maneuver properly, to do it safely, and to do it hundreds if not thousands of times over the course of an air show season, requires one characteristic more than any other.

FOCUS

Focus is the name of the game for that maneuver. Focus like few people are used to. Perhaps the same focus you might have when driving at night, in heavy traffic, in a torrential downpour—that sort of focus. Navy pilots are uniquely suited to fly that particular maneuver, though, because they've all had the opportunity to learn and refine their focus each time they make their approach to landing behind "the boat," the common nickname of any number of 100,000-ton aircraft carriers, the largest ships ever built. Landing on the boat, with an approach speed of 140 knots (165 mph) where the precision required to maintain centerline while the runway constantly moves to the right because of the angled deck aspect of the aircraft carrier and flying an extremely precise 3.5-degree glideslope where going below glideslope could very well result in crashing directly into the back of the boat, takes focus. When you do it at night, it takes even more focus, and it can be absolutely terrifying to those unaccustomed to it. And that's when the weather is good, and both the jet and the boat are operating normally. When the weather degrades, the sea state worsens, the jet has anomalies, the ship has failures, and so on, the process requires not just focus but a level of professionalism from an experienced team that is truly a sight to behold.

That being said, naval aviation doesn't have a monopoly on focus by any stretch. There are a myriad of other jobs and life situations that require similar focus. I share these examples of focus both in Blue Angels air shows and landing onboard the aircraft carrier to illustrate how focus can be learned, it can be taught, and it can be refined to a point almost beyond the belief of the average person. When that level of focus is achieved, a pilot can attain what many consider almost superhuman abilities.

A common question following any Blue Angels air show is, "How much of that show is flown by the computers in the jet?" or something to that effect. Of course, even though our airplane has a fly-by-wire flight control system, not even a single second of the show is flown in any way other than by the hands of the pilots in the formation. The aspect that sets them apart for that hour is their level of focus, leaving many in the crowd wondering if what they just watched was actually real.

That's the same way I feel when I see a wing suit flyer "screaming" through narrow canyons or under bridges; it's the same way most of us feel when we witness the incredible reaction time of a Formula 1 driver. I have a close friend whose brother was a Hall of Fame baseball player, and he commented once that his brother credited his ability to hit better than most to his eyesight—he could actually see the ball as it was leaving the pitcher's hand and therefore knew what pitch he was about to see cross the plate. Eyesight alone of course doesn't send that baseball over the outfield fence; it's the focus that takes place throughout the windup and through the release and over the course of the next ninety feet the ball travels until the perfectly timed swing, both in time and location, makes contact and subsequently wins the big game.

That level of focus is achievable by anyone willing to work for it. One word commonly used both in naval aviation and on the Blue Angels is *compartmentalization*. It's a mouthful of a word, but when understood and properly used, it can function like a wonder drug. The ability to organize your life into compartments—your thoughts, anything vying for your attention in that moment—is absolutely critical to the laser focus I'm discussing. Being able to compartmentalize doesn't happen by accident, though; it's learned through trial and error, through baby steps, and through failure.

When I discuss compartmentalization, I'm always reminded of a scene from a movie I love called *For Love of the Game*, with Kevin Costner playing the role of a major league pitcher in his final game. As you probably guessed from my earlier baseball observation, I've always loved the game, despite never being very good at it myself. I love that it's our national pastime. I love that most little kids play it at one point or another, whether on a little league field or just in their front yard. It's a wonderful game, and it's really *our* game, as American as apple pie and backyard barbecues with family and friends. The scene I'm referring to actually happens a few times throughout the movie. The pitcher takes the mound and is aware of the noise of the crowd, hears the cheers, the boos, the magnitude of what I can only imagine is an overwhelming experience on a major league ballfield, especially in a critical portion of a game. The pitcher, Billy Chapel, stands on the mound, processes the experience, and then says to himself, "Clear the mechanism." In an instant, the whole world goes silent—somewhat akin to putting on a virtual reality headset and feeling like you've just slipped into an alternate reality. Only then, with all his distractions gone, is Billy able to focus and achieve what few others ever could—pitching a perfect game.

As a Blue Angel pilot, I had my "clear the mechanism" moment as well, and it was even a bit more mechanical than the movie depicted it. Each day to start the show, the six pilots would march to their jets, shoulder to shoulder, climb the ladders, and then strap into the fighter with ten separate attachments built into the harness and ejection seat. We typically describe it as "strapping on the jet" because if you truly become one with this incredible machine, it becomes an extension of you both mentally and physically. Rather than being strapped into the jet, this rocket ship is strapped onto you and does as you command.

Once we strapped on the jet and all six of us were set, our senior enlisted maintainer, affectionately known as "Front Man" due in large part to the role he plays during our ground show as the person in front of the audience, would give us the signal by lowering his hand, and we would all simultaneously start our Auxiliary Power Units (which in turn started our engines) and lower our canopies. Despite having been a part of this routine for over ten years and having flown hundreds of air shows in front of millions of spectators, the ground portion could be very nerve-racking. The thought of tripping during the march down or of slipping as I climbed the narrow ladder up the slide of the plane was always present in my thoughts. I was never quite sure what would have been worse: the crowd seeing it and reacting or never hearing the end of it from my so-called friends on the team for the rest of my life (military folks and especially Navy pilots very much enjoy and employ humiliation, good-naturedly of course, as a normal manner of communication). But once that portion was over and the canopies were down and locked, for me, I had cleared the mechanism. Whatever my earlier thoughts or concerns were, whatever I had on my mind that distracted me was now pleasantly gone for the next hour, and it was just me, this incredible machine, and the men and women I trusted more than anyone else on the face of the earth, flying an air show and hopefully motivating and inspiring the future of our great country and military.

Our brains and bodies have a remarkable ability to learn and to teach themselves. It's the only explanation for why someone shooting hoops day after day gets better with every shot taken and, most importantly, with every shot missed. We don't necessarily need a coach telling us what we're doing wrong; we get better just by trying. And failing. And then trying some more. When it comes to compartmentalizing, the same is true. When you find yourself facing a task that requires your total and complete focus but you're unable to do so because your mind is full of other thoughts, there is no better time to make the deliberate effort to focus. The idea of taking your thoughts, your concerns, your distractions, putting them in their own little box, their own little compartment in your brain to be dealt with and addressed later, and then moving on without them weighing you down any longer—that's how you compartmentalize. And likely when you first try it, it won't work—you'll still have some distractions. Your options are naturally to try again or just give up and assume you're not capable of having that level of focus through compartmentalization. Always try again.

In addition to compartmentalization, there are other ways to attain this increased level of focus. One obvious but often disregarded consideration is understanding your physical needs. If you are hungry, exhausted, or uncomfortable, it's much harder to achieve this level of focus. For example, prior to our air shows, our day can have a variety of events. In addition to visits to schools and hospitals and any other tasks on our calendars, Blue Angel pilots are required to work out six days a week due to the nature of flying without a G-suit. These workouts are almost always before the show rather than afterward because the day doesn't typically end until late at night. So, with a morning workout, the pilots must ensure that it's challenging but not so exhausting that they are too tired to fly a physically demanding show that afternoon. We've all had workouts that leave us fatigued to the point where we can't focus on anything. While they might be good in the long run, they're counterproductive for achieving high levels of focus. The trick is to finish energized rather than drained, and this is always at the forefront of our minds during our preshow workouts.

The energy your body derives from food is another key component of achieving an intense level of focus. If you are hungry or thirsty, you'll likely never reach that level of focus because your body is once again focused on addressing your discomfort. As obvious as this might seem, many overlook it, never considering how an energy deficit will affect them later. It takes forethought and planning to ensure you've met your physical needs before the time you know you'll need to focus.

Another equally obvious but often overlooked aspect is that what you're doing needs to involve some level of challenge. If you're attempting to raise your focus level but the activity you're performing is too simple or routine, then you likely won't be able to force yourself to achieve your desired focus. It might just mean you have to add some difficulty or challenge to whatever you're doing to ensure your brain and body are willing to "up their game," so to speak. This basically falls in line with the good stress versus bad stress principle. You're deliberately creating good or positive stress knowing that your mind and body will rise to the occasion and allow you to reach that increased level of focus.

Just like shooting a basketball, if you try again and again, at some point you will realize not only are you doing it but that you're actually quite good at it. That is when you can rid your mind of distractions and achieve the level of focus you had previously thought impossible. The next time you see something that seems unbelievable or almost superhuman, just remember that that person didn't give up when he or she didn't perfect it on their first attempt.

Focus is not reserved to just life-or-death events or adrenaline-fueled activites. Even ordinary actions and interactions can benefit from a high level of focus. A sales pitch to a customer, a critical decision, reading and understanding a contract—all benefit from your ability to focus when needed.

Focus also doesn't necessarily have to be in short bursts, as I've described when landing on the boat at night or during Blue Angel maneuvers. Sometimes it can be a marathon. I took off from the USS *John C. Stennis* on the evening of 6 March 2013 for a close air support mission. Our boat at that time was in the North Arabian Sea (known to us as "the NAS"), and our missions were being flown over Afghanistan (for us, simply AFG). To launch from a carrier in the NAS and fly a mission over AFG, we had to transit for over an hour and cross the entire country of Pakistan before entering AFG airspace. We were never alone, even if we were in a single-seat fighter. Our wingman was always nearby in visual range, and a multitude of other carrier-based fighters and USAF assets departing from a variety of Middle Eastern bases were transiting along the same route at various altitudes and speeds. Having spent almost two years of my life flying up and down what we referred to as the boulevard, I would sometimes hum to myself the song from *Snow White*, "Heigh-ho, Heigh-ho, It's Off to Work We Go," to lighten the mood and forget about the ugliness of what ultimately brought us to the situation we were all in.

But I digress. On that evening, 6 March 2013, I flew along the boulevard with my junior officer wingman for yet another long night spent over Afghanistan. This one wasn't like the rest, though; I asked for this flight for a very specific reason. My wife was being induced to give birth to our third child that day, and I wanted to be able to at least talk to her on the phone at some point during the birth. We had very limited phone access in those days, and just getting a line off the boat was challenging; but for something of that magnitude, I was confident I could get a few minutes to talk with her and share in the emotion of the event. I had asked for that particular flight because it was really the only way I could guarantee that I would be free to talk with her—we were twelve hours ahead, so by the time I landed from our seven- or eight-hour flight, I would be free and without any chance of flying again due to our crew rest requirements following a long mission. As I transited down the boulevard, I typed into my navigation system the GPS coordinates for the hospital where my wife was with our other two children to see just precisely how far away I actually was. As it turned out, I was just a shade under nine thousand nautical miles (nm) away, and the most direct course, according to my nav system, would have been to fly straight over Pakistan and Afghanistan and Russia and even the North Pole on my way to the central valley of California, where our squadron was based and where my family was preparing to grow by one. I went through this exercise in the plane in a very deliberate attempt to allow me to focus. It was my way of identifying the distractions I had: labeling my distraction with a GPS waypoint (WYPT) and then switching the WYPT to where the men and women we were heading to protect were. Eight hours is a long time to be in a very small fighter, and not every moment was full of intensity, so opportunities for distraction were possible. Nonetheless, those on the ground trusted us to be their eyes in the sky and to be at the ready to defend them in any manner of different ways, and I felt strongly that if I wasn't able to compartmentalize and focus, then it wasn't fair to them.

I share this story not because there's anything remarkable about flying while deployed and missing the birth of a child—that's a tale as old as time for military families. I share it in hopes that it provides an example of how not just to avoid distractions but rather to manage them, which is arguably an even more valuable skill. It doesn't take much time or effort to identify possible distractions, and each of us are very capable of coming up with our own solutions. For me, labeling my distraction and switching to a different waypoint was what worked. For you, it will likely be something different. Regardless, determining what your distraction is and then identifying a process to manage or eliminate it will pay off.

Focus, as I've described it, is sometimes referred to as hyperfocus, which medically is viewed somewhat negatively and is often connected to ADHD. The idea of this type of focus is that it allows you to be singularly attuned to a very specific task at hand. The obvious problem or disadvantage of hyperfocus is that you're distracted from other tasks, which might have negative consequences. I'm advocating for the ability to turn it off and on as required by the situation, which is different than having it control you. This ability to "turn on" hyperfocus is often connected with and even confused with a term called *flow state*. Being in a flow state is viewed very favorably because it allows you to both focus on and enjoy the activity to a greater degree. Flow state is often characterized by the extreme level of focus I've described, and it is achieved by setting clear goals, ensuring you're participating in an activity you truly enjoy, and eliminating multitasking.

The term *multitasking* was first used in the 1960s and was intended specifically for computers, but eventually our culture made the leap to human multitasking. At a very basic level, multitasking in the human brain is impossible—what we're actually doing is better known as time slicing. Our brains aren't actually able to do two things at once, but we are able to focus on specific tasks for incredibly short periods of time, measured in milliseconds. When we believe we are multitasking, we are in fact just jumping from one task to the next and then back again in incredibly short periods of time, fractions of a second. What that does to our brain, though, is put a significant load on our cognitive brain function and in turn reduce our ability to focus. I highlight this point because we often view multitasking as a valuable skill and one to be refined, but keep in mind that it's counterproductive if your intent is to increase your level of focus.

The final aspect that allows for the high level of focus I've been describing comes for me through prioritization. A common refrain for getting more organized is to make a list, and in my experience it works. When I feel like I have too much going on, too many balls in the air to juggle at one time, my solution is to make a prioritized list. I write down, in order, what's most pressing, sometimes even what I'm likeliest to forget. It might not be the most important on the list, in some cases the furthest from it, but it is the most pressing because it has a timeline, a suspense that requires it being accomplished.

It also helps me to keep this list focused on immediate priorities, medium priorities, and long-range priorities. I'm using the word *priorities* interchangeably with *tasks* or *items* because, for me, they're one and the same in this case. These are not necessarily scheduled meetings or events; rather, they are items requiring action, precisely what needs to get done. This list is altogether different than a list of priorities for the parts of my life in which I want to improve. That list might include reading more, perhaps even a specific requirement to read a book a week. That same list might also include setting up time to play a musical instrument, learning a new language, staying current on world events, and so on. Naturally that list varies wildly from person to person, but I have found huge benefits in putting these things on paper (or through electronic means on your phone).

Both of these lists combine to make my point about prioritization. There are several great books and articles written about how we prioritize and, moreover, how we use the time we have each day. The point is made that we all have twenty-four hours each day; they are ours to use how we see fit. That "gift" of time is quite possibly our greatest asset and our greatest resource. Despite the astonishing variances in money, net worth, and power that exist all around us, we each have twenty-four hours every day. It doesn't matter if you're a nomadic wanderer in Kazakhstan, a carpenter in South Texas, or Elon Musk; we all have the same amount of that particular resource, that commodity. As you begin to understand that time is really one of the only items distributed evenly across all people, you begin to understand and appreciate its value. It can't be taken from you, and you can't buy more of it, no matter what.

It then follows that how we each use our time is one of the most critical and important decisions we make, and we make that decision daily, if not dozens of times throughout each day. Along those same lines, I suspect we can all admit that we've at various times made comments like, "I didn't do that today; I just didn't have time," which to some degree might be true. Then again, assuming someone else did find time to do whatever that was, then there was of course time to do it—you just chose not to and possibly for a very good reason.

As I work to prioritize my life, I love the exercise of using that expression but switching it around slightly. Instead of simply saying, "I didn't have time," use "That wasn't a priority for me" and see how it goes. For example, "I didn't go to the gym today; I just didn't have time" becomes "I didn't go to the gym today; it wasn't a priority for me." That becomes more honest and may even hurt a bit to say aloud. Or how about, "What a day. . . . I didn't call my mom, and it was her birthday, and I didn't read my daughter a bedtime story; I just didn't have time." If you are brave enough to say you didn't call your mom on her birthday or read your child a bedtime story because neither of them were priorities, then you're a brave individual indeed.

What this does is change how you approach your day and allow you to better prioritize. It becomes an immediate barometer of what's important to you and better allows you to make impactful decisions regarding your most precious resource: your time. I share this concept because the idea of becoming properly prioritized and maintaining that level of prioritization is the most beneficial method of increasing your level of focus. When you find yourself rid of the burden of worrying about what you have on your plate and what balls are up in the air because of your organization and prioritization, it allows for that laser focus I've described.

CHAPTER 2

PERSPECTIVE

"The right perspective makes the impossible possible."

—UNKNOWN

"LEFT! RIGHT! LEFT! Here comes the G!" That's a small portion of what Tom Cruise asked me to say as we were racing through a mountain range southeast of Naval Air Station (NAS) Fallon in Nevada. We were filming the scene that plays about halfway through *Top Gun: Maverick* when his character "borrows" a jet to prove that what he has been asking of the younger pilots is in fact possible.

Tom and I flew through that canyon over and over again until we had it just the way he and the director, Joe Kosinski, wanted it. If you've seen the movie, you've probably noticed that they spared no expense and no detail was too trivial to address. For example, although we flew that canyon run multiple times over multiple days, when you watch the movie you will notice the weather and the environments are always the same—there's perfect continuity in that regard. That certainly wasn't the case in practice, though:

the weather varied significantly from morning to afternoon and from one day to the next.

Paramount released a bit of in-cockpit footage leading up to the movie, and you can see Tom's face as we exit the canyon and hear me say, "It's a bit of a workout," to which he responds, "That's what I'm talking about." As is typical in naval aviation, most of what we do is intentionally downplayed. That canyon run was some of the most intense flying I have ever done, including my ten years of flying with the Blue Angels at very low altitudes and in close formation. It was every bit as intense as the movie depicts it. We were every bit as low as it appears, and every single turn was the highest G turn we could get out of the jet. That was Tom's very clear direction and guidance; he wanted it as dynamic and as intense as possible. His request to me was simply to let him know what was coming up—call my turns and the G in advance so he could ensure he was situating himself in the airplane to bring the most realism possible to the scene. So I did as directed and called the direction slightly in advance of each turn, for the entire canyon, for every single run. I would further add that canyon scene was very much akin to a Blue Angels air show due to its degree of danger and intensity; for that reason we don't allow passengers in our planes on show days. In the case of flying that scene with Tom, because he's such an experienced and accomplished pilot personally, it wasn't as if I had a passenger in the back seat but rather an additional crew member. Tom's air sense and proficiency enabled the flight to be even more dynamic than it would have been were I flying alone.

It's one of my favorite scenes in the movie because I know it's 100 percent real, no special effects, no computer graphics added—I was there and saw it with my own eyes. In fact, no matter how low the plane looks on the big screen or how close the trees appear to be, it certainly felt much closer from inside the jet looking out. That's always the case.

I share the story of that scene because not long ago I was on a flight and the woman next to me was watching the movie. I had a book out and at one point looked up and that particular scene was playing. Pilots, to a large degree, are all just big kids, and it's hard, if not impossible, not to watch anything involving flying. So I didn't immediately look away and rather watched the scene through the canyon. At some point she became aware I was watching, and she hit pause, looked at me, and said, "It's a great movie. You should watch it." I smiled and said, "No, thanks. I'm not really that into aviation." She continued with the movie, and I had a moment of quiet satisfaction knowing she was enjoying it, but I got more satisfaction knowing that only one other person in the whole world knew what that scene looked like from the opposite perspective—that is, what the canyon looked like going straight through it.

The majority of footage from inside a flying airplane in *Top Gun: Maverick* is from cameras installed in the rear cockpit of a two-seat F/A-18F Super Hornet. Those cameras faced aft and were able to get never-before-seen, quality footage of actors flying at low altitudes, in close proximity to other airplanes, and in very dynamic flight environments. It was understood that the actors could act, they could go through their lines and inject the necessary emotion, but even the best actors can't pretend to be inverted or under high G forces. They had to be in the jet while it did all those things and then begin acting. Moreover, because they were alone in the airplane aside from the pilot who was in the front seat, they also functioned as their own director and hair and makeup stylist, and they even drove the pilots around in order to get the best lighting for each scene. It took their normal jobs as actors to an entirely different level.

As I mentioned before, though, when I watch the scenes I was involved in, it is a sort of surreal experience for me because they are not how I remembered them. The scene is looking backward, but I only remember that canyon looking forward. I spent days studying each turn, each mountain ridge, every possible obstruction that could adversely affect our run. I knew it so well I could mentally fly through the entire canyon without ever opening my eyes. I certainly didn't know what it looked like in reverse, though, and that's how it is viewed in the movie. That is the difference we all share in our perspectives, and it's that difference that I want to address.

Perspective is an incredible word; we use it often even if we don't recognize how or when we're using it. The first part of understanding perspective is easy. It's the other part that's hard. Perspective is a person's understanding of ideas and facts, as well as their physical relation to a visible area. If I were to expand on the definition, I would add that it's the position from where one views the world based on one's own experiences, decisions, and subsequent results.

My wife and I call our time in the military our "gift of perspective" because it informs our reactions to everyday life. When we're challenged or stressed, all we have to do is look back and remember eight-month deployments or multiple births when I wasn't home and suddenly everything seems a whole lot easier. Perspective, specifically your perspective, can also be how you approach life. A cancer survivor might be more grateful than expectant. Someone who started with nothing and through hard work and determination became very successful might find obstacles not so daunting. The point is, for all of us over the course of our lifetimes, quite a lot has changed, which shapes our perspectives into something very different.

We all bring our life experiences to bear as we approach each and every day. Our personal perspectives offer us a barometer for measuring our experiences as we live them. They are also constantly changing as we're dealt new and unique challenges and we navigate through our lives.

What affords me constant peace and gratitude is that, even though it doesn't often feel this way, life has gotten a whole lot easier. There's a terrific book by Steven Pinker titled *The Better Angels of Our Nature*. Through the book, Pinker works to explain why violence has declined over the course of human history and civilization. He makes the point early on that for those of us who remember the start of this century—the attacks on 9/11, the wars in Iraq and Afghanistan, the tragedies of Darfur, and so on—it didn't necessarily feel peaceful, but if you compare it to the past and reference that perspective, it does in fact seem a whole lot more peaceful and civilized.

While I was stationed in South Germany working for NATO, I had the opportunity to visit the city of Bolzano in northern Italy. Bolzano, aside from being a beautiful city tucked into the Dolomite Mountains, is home to the Museum of Archaeology, which proudly displays

Ötzi the Iceman as one of its primary exhibits. Ötzi is the oldest natural mummy of a European man who lived from approximately 3275 BC until 3230 BC. His body was discovered by German hikers in 1991 in the South Tyrolean Alps, just north of Bolzano at an elevation of roughly 10,500 feet. Through modern methods, scientists were able to determine what he was wearing, what his last meals were, and even how he died. As it turned out, Ötzi had been shot in the shoulder with an arrow and received multiple blows to his body and head. In short, Ötzi was murdered. I share this story to properly illustrate that the oldest known human who was a part of Western civilization died at the hand of another human, and sadly that has continued for thousands of years. Perspective allows us to understand that throughout our recorded history, there has always been the possibility of catastrophe or threat to life, but the reality is that today we are far safer than at any point in our past.

That perspective brings me reassurance when it seems that we're surrounded by violence. Not only is the world safer, but in fact it's easier in really every measurable way. Recognizing that can once again help us to be grateful rather than frustrated.

I've found that putting myself into challenging situations, whether mentally or physically, or conditions that might involve some level of suffering, can be extremely beneficial to enhancing my perspective and in turn to my appreciating life even more. Suffering sounds a bit extreme, but I don't mean it to be. Let me give you an example.

As a young man I was in the Boy Scouts. I joined Troop 463 in Atlanta specifically because they made a commitment to go backpacking one weekend every month. Neither of my parents are what you would call outdoorsy, so I didn't receive much in the form of advice or tutelage prior to my first backpacking trip. To say I made mistakes would be a massive understatement. To start, I didn't have a backpack, which as you might expect is one of the more critical aspects of going backpacking. So I sold a bunch of tickets to the annual Scout Show (akin to the Girl Scout cookie fundraisers), and in return for my ticket sales, I "won" a backpack. This wasn't the backpack you'd expect to see on someone who knows what they're doing in the woods. This was a large nylon garbage bag, no pockets, no padded straps, and with a drawstring at the top. In fact, the straps that went over my shoulders were the thinnest and cheapest webbing you could find and were far less padded than even your traditional grade school backpack meant for holding a book or two—definitely not intended to hold everything you need for a weekend in the mountains.

Being the novice I was, I loaded my new pack totally full of everything I might need; and then because I was a Boy Scout and well aware of our motto to "be prepared," I put a bunch of other stuff in there too, just in case. Off we went the next morning on an easy five-mile (two-hour) hike to our campsite in the Cohutta Wilderness of North Georgia. I was a reasonably tough thirteen-year-old, not keen to show weakness in front of my peers, certainly not the older scouts. But all that went out the window about fifteen minutes into the hike as the thin straps of the ridiculously poorly packed and heavy backpack dug into my bony shoulders. Pride went first, and fast, and next it was downright begging on my part to see who wanted to trade, even for just a few minutes. I offered any sweets I had, water, ultimately even my dinner just to make the pain go away. Sadly for me, the misery didn't end there.

Not owning a tent, I had borrowed one from an uncle and even practiced setting it up in my backyard because, of course, it was critical to be prepared. Unfortunately, the flat backyard of our suburban Atlanta house was not an accurate representation of the hill we eventually decided to call our campsite for the night, and although I set up the tent nearly perfectly, it didn't become apparent until it was dark and I climbed into my sleeping bag that I had pitched the tent on the side of a rather steep hill. I immediately rolled over on top of my tent mate. To summarize, I had a brutally painful hike with tired legs and raw shoulders, traded away my dinner and dessert, and spent a sleepless night in a sleeping bag lying on top of a friend and moving every few minutes up the hill only to roll back down, all followed by a hike back to our cars the following morning. The wonderful thing about perspective, though, is that even a few years later, after many trips into the woods with my scout troop, I remembered fondly that "at least it wasn't raining."

The gift of perspective allows us to appreciate life and to be grateful rather than entitled. It allows us to remember a time when perhaps life was harder, and having survived those times, we find ourselves both stronger and more able to conquer the challenges of today.

My camping adventures weren't over after the Boy Scouts. As someone who learned a love of the outdoors through the Boy Scouts, I found myself running the Mountaineering Club for the Naval Academy and turning my attention to bigger mountains than what North Georgia offered. My love for the mountains took me all over the

United States, to climb Denali in Alaska and even to drag my then-girlfriend to the top of Mount Kilimanjaro in Tanzania where I asked her to marry me. The gift of perspective was immediately hers as climbing to the highest point in Africa paled in comparison to the challenges that lay ahead for our family's time serving our country. Military families routinely joke, mostly because it's true, that the minute the service member leaves on deployment, the washing machine breaks, a roof leak unexpectedly appears, and all the kids are instantly sick, and the spouse is now alone to handle the myriad issues that have arisen. This was certainly the case for our family on each and every deployment, and military spouses do a truly incredible job joining forces and helping each other survive the trials and tribulations of being alone while their spouse is deployed.

Following flight school, military personnel are required to spend two weeks at SERE school before deployment. SERE stands for Survival, Evasion, Resistance, and Escape, and the mission of SERE school is to train those who will deploy into combat areas how to do all four. If you find yourself, for example, ejecting over enemy territory, the first step is to Survive. If you can manage that, the next step is to Evade. If that doesn't go as planned and you're captured, the Resistance portion refers to not immediately spilling your guts and offering up every single thing you know about tactics, operations, and so on. Finally, it's imperative that any captured POW always be planning for an eventual Escape when possible.

There's a lot more to SERE school, and there have been plenty of books written solely about this topic. Quite frankly, saying it's an unpleasant experience elicits laughs among those who have attended as they all remember vividly just how miserable the training period is. After a week of classroom instruction, all the students are sent out into woods to spend the next week with nothing to eat and only the shelters they're able to construct for their relief from the elements. Students are paired up with a partner while they practice their skills of survival, evasion, resistance, and escape. My partner was a young, strong Marine preparing for his first deployment. Despite his youth and intensity, he'd spent very little time outdoors and certainly wasn't ready for the cold, the rain, and the lack of food. Thankfully, because of my childhood time spent in exactly those conditions, I reveled in the experience and likened it to the camping trips of my youth, which I thought I might never again enjoy. The resistance and escape portions were wholly less enjoyable, but I'll save those stories for another time. We often don't realize how these unpleasant and difficult experiences slowly and steadily mold our character and ultimately provide great purpose to our lives. This is, once again, the gift of perspective.

I share this experience in the spirit of illustrating the benefits of perspective. If we remain cognizant of where we've come from, it empowers us along the path to where we're going. It affirms our confidence, strengthens our resolve, and allows for a life of gratitude.

Most important, though, is a different kind of perspective. The examples of SERE school and camping very much focus on my personal perspective and how it was changed by my life experiences. What I really want to address is everyone else's perspectives. That is to say, rather than focusing on our own perspectives, we must put ourselves in the shoes of those around us and endeavor to understand and appreciate their perspectives, which informs how we interact with them. A great definition of perspective is intertwined with the word *empathy*. I notice that a lot of people regularly confuse sympathy and empathy. To quickly explain, sympathy is acknowledging someone's pain and feeling sorry for their situation, while empathy means putting yourself in their position and genuinely connecting with their emotions. Phrased a different way, recognizing someone else's perspective means being truly empathetic and "walking a mile in their shoes."

The Blue Angels focus on the perspectives of others better than most organizations because it's the absolute backbone of our mission. We use our jets to perform for a group of spectators, so our perspective isn't the important one—it's the spectator's perspective that matters. How does this manifest itself in our show? Let me explain.

I described the Solo takeoff maneuver in the last chapter. As the show continues, the Solo pilots immediately fly to opposite sides of our airspace, which is typically a three-dimensional cylinder that goes from the surface up to 15,000 feet from the center of the show outboard, with a radius of 5 nautical miles (nm). The Solo pilots begin the first maneuver, the Opposing Knife Edge Pass, approximately 9.5 nm apart from one another. It's up to the Solo pilots to manage the timing of the show and ensure there's an appropriate amount of downtime between maneuvers. This allows for the music and narration and, most importantly, minimizes the downtime to prevent the spectators from losing interest. Each maneuver very deliberately begins based off the timing of the Blue Angel Diamond. The Blue Angel

Diamond consists of Blue Angel #1 (the flight leader and commanding officer of the squadron), Blue Angel #2 (the right wingman), Blue Angel #3 (the left wingman), and Blue Angel #4 (the slot pilot who flies directly below and behind the flight lead). This formation is essentially fixed in their timing as they fly their required profile, and the Solo pilots adjust to reset the timing after each maneuver.

Following the Diamond's takeoff maneuver, they turn in for the next maneuver, the Diamond 360, which is intended to showcase the precise formation capabilities of the aircraft. In this maneuver, the wingmen get so incredibly close that Blue Angel #4, flying below the other aircraft, could grab the near wingtips of both Blue Angels #2 and #3 from his seated position if the canopy weren't in the way. It's so incredibly close that it takes the breath away from even career fighter pilots when they're offered a ride in the back seat of the #4 jet. To fly this maneuver properly, Blue Angel #1 has to fly an exceptionally smooth and predictable profile to allow the wingmen to tighten up to that degree. Knowing the difficulty and level of risk, it would bring a smile to my face as we converged on air show center, flying over the crowd in that breathtaking, iconic Blue Angel formation.

There's not much time to appreciate the Diamond, though, as we began our next maneuver with the resetting of a stopwatch bolted to our heads-up display with a plan to cross over show center exactly 47 seconds later. The Solo pilots deliberately fly at exactly 400 knots so they cover exactly 1 nm every 9 seconds. We use very precise checkpoints on the ground to ensure our timing is accurate because the goal is to cross over center point, and our desired tolerance is no more than 100 feet either left or right. At that speed, if either jet is off their timing by even a quarter of a second, it moves the cross by 167 feet. That means the allowable error is approximately one-seventh of a second, or one-fourteenth of a second per pilot (assuming the errors don't cancel each other out).

To fly the jets to that level of accuracy, precise checkpoints and airspeed control are critical. If the Opposing Solo reports being a quarter of second ahead, the Lead Solo correspondingly reduces speed by 5 knots to 395 knots for the next 2 miles, then accelerates back to 400 knots immediately before the cross. Assuming #6 flies precisely 400 knots, the two jets will cross directly over the center point. It's not actually quite that easy, though, as the wind has a way of complicating flying in a variety of ways. The speed of the aircraft isn't in fact relevant at all—it's the speed over the ground, commonly referred to as ground speed, that matters. The jets are each flying independently through a moving air mass, and if that air mass is moving from left to right at 10 knots, then the jet ingressing from the left needs to actually fly 390 knots while the aircraft ingressing from the right has to fly 410 knots to account for the wind.

All those corrections are required for a center point cross, but the location of the cross is only half of the equation and perhaps less important than even that. The precise altitude of the jets as they cross in front of the crowd is really what makes or breaks the maneuver. The intent of the maneuver is to have the jets cross so their noses look to be at exactly the same altitude, but unfortunately, it's not as simple as just flying at the same altitude.

Geometry is the name of the game for a perfect cross, so it goes back to our days of memorizing the Pythagorean theorem and studying trigonometry. Picture yourself standing among 100,000 spectators waiting for the jets to cross. If you're an average American, you're between 5′5″and 5′10″, and the jets generally cross 1,200 to 1,500 feet away from the spectators. If the Lead Solo flies 200 feet over the ground, then the Opposing Solo pilot must compute his required altitude by determining the distance from the crowd, the altitude of the Lead Solo, and their separation from each other. For example, with a center point distance of 1,500 feet, a Lead Solo at 200 feet, and 100 feet between them at the cross, then the Opposing Solo would need to fly at an altitude of 213 feet; and unfortunately our altimeter only shows every 10 feet. If, however, the center point distance was 1,200 feet and it was later in the show season after they lowered their altitudes so the Lead Solo was flying at an altitude of 100 feet, then the Opposing Solo would be only 50 feet away at the cross and the new altitude required would be 104 feet. That likely made your head hurt, so I apologize. When a child asked me how we did it, it always provided an opportunity to explain the importance of math. My own kids never appreciated me telling them that my greatest preparation to becoming a fighter pilot and Blue Angel was being a math major, even if they knew I was mostly joking.

Now that you understand the flight aspects required to set up the cross and the math required to be done while flying, we can get to the most important part of that maneuver, the perfect cross. Let's say the Lead Solo recalls flying the exact prebriefed parameters, and the Opposing Solo believes he also flew precisely the right distance and altitude to set up the perfect cross. Hours later in the debrief room, the pilots watch the video of the demonstration, which is deliberately filmed from the center of the spectators so the pilots can see, for the first time, the show as the crowd saw it. While watching the debrief tape, they notice that the cross wasn't in fact perfect but rather that #6 looked slightly high—the maneuver wasn't flown as intended.

Having served with and flown with the Blue Angels for over ten years of my Navy career, the lessons learned from that aspect alone have had a tremendous impact on my life. At the most basic level, the personal perspective of each pilot during a Blue Angels show is only partially important; the spectator's perspective is of the utmost importance.

What if you went about your day, your job, your interactions with others and you focused your efforts not on yourself and your own perspective but rather on the perspectives of those around you? It's a fairly simple concept but in practice it can prove quite difficult. It boils down to being concerned about the effect you have on others rather than the effect they have on you. I read Dale Carnegie's book *How to Win Friends and Influence People* as a child, and it was unquestionably the most life-changing book I have ever read. It basically makes this exact point but in a variety of different ways. Carnegie famously points out that the best conversationalists are the ones who do almost no talking and focus entirely on listening. Most people are so excited to talk about themselves that simply being interested and engaged makes you the most enjoyable person to talk to. That is to say, you're focused on their perspective and want them say what's on their mind so you can see things from their vantage point. You might have a lot you want to share as well, but recognizing the importance of their perspective, you remain quiet, and in return you're viewed as an exceptional conversationalist. To distill it down even further: interesting people are interested.

Toward the end of my career, I had the privilege of flying in a variety of scenes for the movie *Top Gun: Maverick*. My involvement began because of my time flying at low altitude with the Blue Angels because the storyline for the movie required jets flying at extremely low altitudes. As the story was told to me, the movie's leadership was discussing with Navy leadership what would be required, and one scene in particular needed a Super Hornet to be flown at 10 to 20 feet off the ground. This posed a problem because traditionally in the Navy, jets are flown *much* higher than that, even when operating in a low-altitude environment. To add a bit of perspective, for fighter pilots who haven't flown in a low-altitude environment recently, the minimum altitude (MINALT) for that flight is 500 feet above ground level (AGL). Once the pilot is proficient, meaning they've flown in the low-altitude environment a certain number of times over a certain period, they can fly lower, down to 200 feet AGL. Prior to those flights, the pilots involved will be briefed on the dangers and risks associated with low-level flying. Specifically, they'll brief their Mission Crosscheck time, which refers to the amount of time the pilot can glance inside the cockpit rather than keeping their eyes outside and on the horizon. This is critical as the lion's share of their attention needs to be outside the cockpit as the greatest risks are the terrain, obstructions, birds, and so on. So looking inside to change the radio frequencies, update the navigation system, or adjust the weapon system is limited to a prebriefed amount of time.

The closest example to this in everyday life is becoming distracted with a cell phone while driving despite the risks of the cars and road conditions around you. When a fighter pilot is at 200 feet AGL and in a turn, the mission crosscheck time allowed to look inside is one second. That's it. Any more than that can be deadly and risk loss of aircraft and/or life. So if the mission crosscheck time is one second at 200 feet, it's nonexistent between 10 and 20 feet AGL. The whole idea, and certainly the way the Blue Angels operate, is that there's no option or possibility of looking inside when you're at that low of an altitude. If any reason arises that would necessitate looking inside, for example an alert or caution is activated, before ever glancing inside, the first course of action is to climb and to do so quickly. Gaining altitude can buy you time to think and to troubleshoot, so that's always the first step.

Fighter pilots also have rules about flying at low altitude, and one of them, which seems counterintuitive to many, is that you must fly fast, usually upwards of 350–400 knots. The simple reason is that speed can be exchanged for altitude by translating your kinetic energy (think airspeed) to potential energy (think altitude). This is akin to riding a bike down a hill. At the top of the hill you're not moving but you have a great deal of potential energy, and with no effort at all you'll accelerate going downhill. At the bottom of the hill you don't have any more potential energy but you have a great deal of kinetic energy in terms of your speed, so you can trade that by going up the next hill without even pedaling. That concept works the same for flying. We recognize something is wrong and immediately trade that speed for altitude, which removes us from the flight regime with the most danger and gets us to a safe altitude to troubleshoot the issue.

For the scenes requiring a jet be flown at extremely low altitudes, using an experienced Blue Angels pilot—with hundreds of hours and thousands of low-altitude air show demonstrations under their belt—was an easy decision. And thus began my involvement. The level of acceptable risk for the Navy to participate in making *Top Gun: Maverick* was decidedly low for a number of obvious reasons. First and foremost, it's a movie, so it's nice to have, not need to have. When our men and women are in combat and under fire, that level of acceptable risk rises substantially, and we will support them with almost no immediate thought to the risk involved past operating our jet safely and professionally. For the movie, however, there wasn't an appetite to risk losing a jet or aircrew just to make it look good on the big screen. So in an effort to minimize the risk, the Navy chose to use its experts in each phase of flight to assist in the production. This means that when they filmed the dogfighting scenes, they used TOPGUN instructors who are unquestionably the best and most proficient in that type of flying. For the scenes shot on and around the aircraft carrier, they used the carrier landing instructors from our Fleet Replacement Squadron, and so on. For the extremely low-altitude and inverted scenes, I flew to ensure we had an appropriate amount of experience in those flight regimes.

Early in the filming, one of the proposed scenes that received the most attention from naval aviation leadership was a scene to be shot at an extremely low altitude over the high desert just east of Fallon, Nevada, where the TOPGUN facility and training range is located. From a flying perspective the scene is quite easy: just fly low and straight and don't hit the film crew. Nothing to it, right? Flying low isn't any harder than flying high; any pilot can do it. The only catch is that the risk level is significantly elevated due to the proximity to the ground. When max performed, Super Hornets can achieve climb and descent rates of 50,000 feet per minute, so even a small unintentional stick input could cause the jet to descend those 10 feet in a fraction of a second. Because of that high degree of risk, the head of naval aviation at that time, Vice Adm. DeWolfe "Bullet" Miller, required that I have a phone brief with him before and after each flight.

One of the methods I used to mitigate the risks involved was to tie in the manned flight simulator (MFS) at NAS Patuxent River in Maryland, the home of the Navy's test pilots. Their simulator is far more advanced than a traditional F/A-18 simulator, and the primary operator of it is Dr. Steve Naylor, who has a doctorate in the laser-based velocity measurement of fluid flow. That alone should demonstrate what the simulator and its operators can create and achieve. The MFS can provide an incredibly realistic simulation both with its graphics and with the aircraft's response. We were able to set up the exact location where the filming would take place and simulate the environments in addition to the correct graphics. This aspect is critical because the altitude in a high desert alone causes the aircraft to respond significantly different than it would at sea level. Airplanes are much like our bodies, and just like it's harder to run a mile in Denver, Colorado, at 5,000 feet elevation, the airplane doesn't perform as well at higher altitudes either. We wanted to replicate the flight as accurately as possible, and the MFS enabled us to do exactly that. The other huge advantage of the MFS is that because we were using it for Blue Angel transition testing as we moved from the Legacy F/A-18 A–D models to the Super Hornet (E–F models), we had already installed the spring (Artificial Feel Spring) I mentioned last chapter. That spring removes any ambiguity in the controls and allows the pilot to have total and complete positive control over the aircraft's movement. So we set up the scene just as it was to be flown and ran through dozens of iterations at various fuel states and weather conditions. We even added some emergencies just to make sure we would be prepared and ready to go the day the filming took place.

On the day of filming, we found ourselves in Fallon, Nevada, and we briefed the flight, the range space used, the approximate location of the film crew, and more. The crew on-site had a far more challenging journey than I did because the location was only 20 nm from the base, so the flight itself was less than five minutes. Meanwhile, vans packed with people and cameras and equipment loaded up and headed east on Hwy 50 to eventually depart the highway and transition to small dune buggies that were necessary to cover the inhospitable desert terrain. I took off from Fallon, located their position, and noted that it wasn't the precise location we'd briefed because they found a spot that was more conducive to setting up their equipment while managing the sun angles and other relevant environmental factors. I entered their approximate position by "dropping a mark" on them, a procedure we use in the F/A-18 to denote ground reference points. It's accurate in certain cases, but depending on the altitude, exact speed, and time when you drop the mark, the "mark" could still be a good distance away from where you intended it to be. Nonetheless, I had a rough idea of their location, so I flew downwind to set up for our first pass.

The trick to doing this properly is, first, do not hit the ground (of course), and, second, find the film crew and fly directly over them. That might not sound terribly challenging, but as it turns out, it's not as easy as you might think. The Salt Flats of the Fallon Range complex leave a bit to be desired in terms of "ground gouge" or anything that gives you a sense of where you are. What I mean is there are no roads, no discernable features, literally nothing but sand. I had the crew's approximate position, so I proceeded downwind. The brief was for me to proceed to about 12 nm away, then turn back and descend so I would be down at my low altitude and heading their way from 8 to 10 nm away. The intent of this scene was described as the *Top Gun: Maverick* version of *Lawrence of Arabia*, but rather than a dot in the distance slowly turning into a man on a camel, that dot in the distance would quickly turn into a dust cloud that turned into a fighter at near-supersonic speed directly overhead.

While I was able to pin down the first aspect of the trick to doing this properly, do not hit the ground, the second part, find the film crew, was proving harder than expected. At that low altitude, your ability to see where you're going is almost as if you were standing on the ground yourself; you lose the benefit of being elevated and therefore of seeing farther. If you were on opposite ends of a football field from someone, nominally 300 feet apart, you could certainly see that other human being, or in this case a film crew with a dozen people and their cameras. However, if you're 10 nautical miles away, which is 60,000 feet, it's significantly harder to see someone; and for me, it's impossible. So I pointed in the direction I believed they were, descended, accelerated, and did my level best to fly a stable jet for the first attempt. As it turned out, through sheer luck, I flew directly over them! I for one was totally elated, since much of the time inbound, I had already anticipated being a mile or two north or south and never hearing the end of it from the gang when the flight was over. I had even pictured the conversations taking place, with the director leaning over to his producer and saying, "Where'd they find this idiot?" Thankfully, though, it's always better to be lucky than good, and I benefited from a great deal of luck. As I climbed up and proceeded to turn downwind to set it up again, I was overcome with glee that I hadn't screwed it up and was quite proud of myself for finding them at all. In the midst of that little aviation high I was experiencing, the aerial film coordinator, Kevin "K2" Larosa, who was on a radio frequency with me, said, "Hey, Walleye. I know how this is gonna sound, but the director is asking that if on the next pass you wouldn't mind coming about a foot further to the right."

So we find ourselves back to the subject of perspective. From my perspective, I was overjoyed at even finding this small group of folks in the middle of the desert while flying my airplane mere feet off the ground at near-supersonic speeds. From the director's perspective, meanwhile, the plane hadn't perfectly filled their camera lens, and to get the shot I would need to be one foot to the right. The problem with that, though, is you can't turn your jet at that altitude. When you effect a turn, the corresponding wing drops while the opposite wing rises, which causes the aircraft to turn. If I had tried that, the wing would have certainly hit the ground. The other, less used option in fighters is to use the rudders. You can depress the corresponding rudder pedal, and the aircraft essentially laterally shifts in that direction without actually changing course. However, the problem with that option is that at the speeds I was flying, merely *looking* at the rudder pedal would have caused the jet to translate 50 feet if not a 100 feet in an instant, so that wasn't a viable solution either.

I resigned myself to just making as many safe passes as I could given my fuel load and the conditions, and my hope was that one of them would have my jet squarely in the director's lens. I flew close to a dozen low passes and felt very comfortable with how the jet handled and the feedback I received. After I landed, we debriefed, and while that happened, people began airdropping to the group the pictures they had taken that day on their phones. There was one picture in particular that caught my eye, and when I inquired about what was going on, I was told, "Oh, we got the shot we needed pretty early on, but we had you keep doing the low passes so we could all get selfies." (We'll cover *trust* in the next chapter.)

We're left with this perspective issue. My perspective was that I was trying my best to fly the perfect and safest profile and earn the trust of the film crew. Their perspective was that I was good to go, they got the shot they wanted, and now they wanted to immortalize what was an incredible day for the Paramount crew (and me!) in the

Fallon Range complex by getting selfies to remember the experience.

I've explained the benefits of being empathetic and trying to truly understand someone else's perspective. Let me give you an example of what happens when you don't make that effort. My first year on the Blue Angels, I was #7 and was the Narrator for the air show. My flying job was to conduct our VIP flights for backseat riders. It wasn't nearly as challenging or exacting as flying the air show demonstration, but the profile we would fly was very similar to the Lead Solo pilot profile, albeit at much higher altitudes and without another aircraft crossing with high closure rates and minimum separation. That said, it really allowed me to get comfortable flying the jet and learning our procedures; and on top of all that, it was rewarding to fly with some really incredible people over the course of that year.

We mixed up who received rides in the back seat, but celebrities and athletes were invited in some cases because they could generate, just by existing, their own media. For the Blue Angels, that sort of media and impressions was what we were targeting. For example, one of my rides during our winter training period was with Tim Wakefield, a knuckleballer and two-time World Series champion. I remember Tim mentioning that his father had been a fighter pilot in Vietnam, and he was excited to fly in a Blue Angels jet. We had an incredible time together; he did exceptionally well in the jet. And when we landed, New England Sports Network was there to capture a postflight interview. When asked how the flight compared to winning the World Series, he said, "It doesn't. I should have done this for a living!" Having someone who millions of young people idolize say that is worth more than a year of advertising for the Navy, and that's the prime reason we conduct those types of flights.

One of the most interesting things I learned that year was that you can never really tell in advance how someone is going to do in the jet. I flew with some of the most physically imposing and impressive people on the planet: NFL Hall of Famers, MMA fighters, gold medal Olympic wrestlers—the list goes on. In many cases, they were outperformed in the jet by a quiet and reserved sixty-year-old female guidance counselor who turned out to be an absolute G monster who loved every second of the flight. For me it quickly became less about the celebrity or notoriety of the rider and more about how well they did and how much they enjoyed the flight. What was unexpectedly wonderful about the job was that I had flown thousands of hours at that point and in many cases conducted almost the same flight profile each day, but my rider was always on their first and only ride, and that allowed me to experience the excitement anew each and every flight. It was a magical year in aviation for me.

In addition to giving backseat rides, I would travel in advance of the team to each air show to handle the setup and logistics. With me in my two-seat Hornet was the #7 crew chief, a Navy sailor or Marine who had been selected as the crew chief for the #7 jet. It was a prestigious position because the #7 Geek (as he or she was called) got to fly in the jet every week and be the point person for all maintenance-related items with the air show.

I had two crew chiefs that first season who would alternate weeks—one was a Marine E-6 whose training was in powerplants, or our engines, and the other was a Navy E-6 petty officer whose specialty was in ejection seats and our pressurization system. Each sailor and Marine on the Blue Angels would get one backseat ride during their three- or four-year tour, but the #7 Geeks had close to fifty rides by the time their tour was over, so they got quite comfortable in the jet, which helped them better brief our backseat riders prior to their flights.

A somewhat typical stereotype between the pilots and the maintainers is that the pilots are showboats who get the attention while the maintainers do all the hard work and never really get the grease out from under their fingernails. There's truth to these stereotypes for sure, but there are always exceptions and, importantly, there is an incredibly strong level of mutual respect between the groups.

I had returned from a maintenance flight on the #7 jet one afternoon, and my #7 Geek happened to be in the maintenance control room when I walked through. We would pass through there after each flight to fill out our flight times and note any discrepancies. I mentioned that there was a somewhat noxious smell of oil early on in the flight, but it dissipated over time. I told him it would be nice to get it fixed, but it wasn't a "downing discrepancy" in my opinion, which meant the jet could fly safely without it being fixed. Staff Sergeant Crew Chief Deo Harrypersaud, my #7 Geek, looked at me with his typical grin and raised eyebrow and said sarcastically, "Really, sir? Did it not smell nice while you were flying your jet around?" with a bit of a snicker. I said something to the effect of, "Well, I guess you'll find out tomorrow," because we were leaving first thing the next morning to fly to our next show.

Truth be told, I believe we both fully forgot about it by the next morning, and we manned up for our flight. Deo loved to fly, so it was fairly typical after getting airborne and raising the gear and the flaps that I would immediately pass the controls to him, and he would fly us almost the entire way to our destination. He got incredibly good at flying the jet over his time on the Blue Angels. That morning, everything was the same: we lifted off, cleaned up the jet, and I said, "Your jet, Deo." But on this particular day, he coughed back, "Holy shit, sir. What is going on with the fumes?" In his opinion, the noxious gas smell was so bad and overpowering that he wasn't able to fly and was in a full-on coughing fit in the back seat. I graciously responded, "Oh, does it not smell nice flying your jet this morning?"

Thankfully the fumes went away shortly thereafter, as they had the day before, and the rest of the flight was uneventful. I share this story not to dog on Deo, but to underline the power of perspective. Had Deo been willing to entertain my perspective the day prior, being that engines were his specialty, he could have fixed the problem in no time at all. The real benefit for me, though, was the instant credibility it provided me as someone who hadn't complained and merely said it was uncomfortable but manageable, whereas Deo found it absolutely miserable. Because of the subsequently changed perspective, I benefited the rest of the season—when I griped about some aspect of the jet, it was dealt with accordingly and with far less mockery.

Why does all this matter? Because if you're able to truly appreciate someone else's perspective, you instantly become an empathetic boss, supervisor, teammate, or subordinate. In fact, if you make the effort to reorient yourself to others' perspectives, I submit that you will find renewed purpose and a connection with those around you that you've never before been able to achieve. It's not magic; it's just a mind shift that comes with deliberate effort.

CHAPTER 3

TRUST

"The best way to find out if you can trust somebody is to trust them."

—ERNEST HEMINGWAY

TWENTY SECONDS PRIOR to landing, I transmitted, "301, Hornet Ball; 5.6. No HUD [heads-up display]." The carrier landing signal officer (LSO) immediately responded with, "Roger, Ball. No HUD; you're on glide slope." It seems like things always go wrong when you're flying off the carrier at night and the weather sucks. I'm sure it's not entirely true, but it does feel that way.

We were onboard the USS *John C. Stennis* and on our way to the Persian Gulf. It takes almost a full month to sail from the coast of California to the Middle East onboard a carrier; and that's with only a few stops for liberty and to resupply along the way. During those transits, flying isn't always the priority—getting to the destination is. That said, it's still both useful and required to have a few fly days each week to stay proficient and execute training missions to prepare for the upcoming combat flights.

On this particular night, I was flying a division self-escort strike along with my roommate and lifelong friend Tom "Nemo" Hoyt and two other pilots from our sister squadron. There were a number of jets from other squadrons simulating the enemy, or aggressor, to ensure we received accurate training. As was often the case, our somewhat old F/A-18s had some maintenance issues, and traditionally we give those jets to the senior pilots in the squadron. One way the various squadrons compete and distinguish themselves is by maintaining a high sortie completion percentage, meaning they don't cancel flights for maintenance problems. As a pilot becomes more senior and gains more experience in the jet, he or she gets better at troubleshooting and more comfortable flying in planes that have a few gremlins—our term for known issues. On this night, my jet had been having electrical issues we couldn't seem to pinpoint and fix; but it wasn't every flight, and it wasn't obvious what was causing them. So off we went to rendezvous for the simulated airborne battle, and no sooner had I gotten to the rendezvous point when one of my displays started to flicker. That was soon followed by a light indicating my right generator had failed, which was almost immediately followed by the HUD powering off.

I transmitted what I was seeing to Nemo, who had flown that jet recently and knew about its issues. We both agreed that I should return to the carrier and try to land before the previous cycle finished up rather than staying airborne for the next ninety minutes and giving the jet more time to fall apart. I stayed on the strike team's frequency on my second radio while I checked in with the controllers on the first and explained my situation. As I flew toward the boat and talked to the various controllers and squadron reps regarding what was happening in my cockpit, more displays started powering off. Nemo at some point checked in to see how I was doing, and I told him what had transpired. He didn't waste a second; he turned away from the airborne battle and immediately started running me down from almost 30 nm in trail.

At that point, of the normal four displays, only one remained on, and I wasn't sure if it was giving me accurate information because the radar altimeter (which tells us our height over the ground, or water in this case) had failed and the radio navigation equipment that allows us to find the carrier was also intermittent and quickly becoming useless. I spent the fifteen-minute flight back to the boat giving a rundown of what was failing in the jet to a fellow squadron department head, Matt "TOD" Doyle, and informing him that Nemo was en route to my position. If you lose all the avionics in your plane at night, the traditional method for landing is to fly formation with another airplane. The fully functional jet flies lead and lines up as if he is landing. He lowers his landing gear, flaps, and arresting hook at prebriefed times to ensure the airplane is properly configured to land. He also flies the precise course and glide slope to land on the carrier with the "hurt bird" on his right wing. At roughly 3/4 nm from the carrier, the lead pilot will make sure the follow pilot has the carrier in sight, and then he will break away, allowing the malfunctioning jet to land. For the pilot flying formation, this is a somewhat challenging routine: you must transition from close-formation flying to very precise "ball flying," meaning scanning the carrier landing area for your lineup left and right, watching your glide slope up and down, and monitoring your speed. Most pilots immediately diverge from one or more aspects of their approach during the changeover, and then there's no more elegance involved; it's land the airplane safely and just get on deck.

Aware of how challenging this landing can be and also considering that one of my displays was still working, I told Nemo I would prefer to fly the approach myself using my limited avionics and visual references, restricted as they are at night, and have him fly on my wing to back me up. My request to do this was somewhat abnormal and was a lot to ask of another pilot; were it not Nemo, someone I knew to be incredibly talented in the jet, I wouldn't have requested this option. It required that he both fly formation and scan all his various displays to ensure I was on the proper course, glide slope, and speed. Doing this during the daytime over land is hard; doing this at night, at low altitude, and onto an aircraft carrier makes it far more challenging.

For both Nemo and me, this was hardly a notable flight over the course of an eight-month combat deployment. We still had plenty of more challenging and critical flights in front of us, but I share this story because it was possible only through trust. I'd known Nemo since we were Plebes at the Naval Academy. We'd flown together many times, and we knew each other's capabilities. He trusted that I wouldn't get so far out of parameters that I would put us both in a dangerous situation, and I trusted him with my life. I trusted that he was both able and willing to fly on my wing low over the water at night while still scanning his instruments as if he were the one landing. If he had made a mistake or misjudged our course or altitude, we both could have ended up in the water that night. That level of trust can't be found just anywhere. It must be built and earned, and is the type of trust I want to discuss with you. It's not limited only to naval aviation or the military—it surrounds us in all we do if we're willing to work toward it.

Trust is like perspective in that it's a word we know and use every day. In fact, we probably use it so frequently we even forget what it truly means. Additionally, trust has so many various definitions that we likely all think it means something slightly different.

Merriam-Webster defines *trust* as "assured reliance on the character, ability, strength, or truth of someone or something; one in which confidence is placed." Another definition says it's the obligation or responsibility imposed on a person in whom confidence or authority is placed. But those both refer to trust as a noun. If we address *trust* as a verb, then it means "to rely on the truthfulness or accuracy of; or to place confidence in" someone or something.[1] As it turns out, despite all the various meanings and uses for the word *trust*, the word that is most prevalent in all the definitions is *confidence*. I can say beyond a shadow of a doubt, that dark night in the Western Pacific, I had full confidence in Nemo to help me land safely.

The act of trusting others requires both being honest and being vulnerable. The first step toward that is honor, because if you don't have personal honor, you aren't truly able to trust anyone. Those who lack the ability to be honest lack it both inwardly and outwardly. Those who cannot be honest with others are most certainly not honest with themselves. Their other undoing is that they, whether they want to or not, project that dishonesty onto those around them.

While I was flying air shows with the Blue Angels, we pilots were sent to talk to young adults each Friday morning in the various cities in which we were performing. Typically, at least during the school year, we would go to high schools in the surrounding areas. Other times we went to trade schools, civic organizations, and the like. We would show a video that included our performances, cockpit footage, and stories from our sailors, and we would then use it as a springboard to jump into our presentation. We weren't there to sign them up to serve our country; we were there to explain why we chose to do so and share some of our experiences. I routinely used an example of two buildings when I was giving my presentations, and it went something like this.

I would use the city they lived in as an example and ask for audience help to determine the two highest buildings in their downtown. I would then explain my (hypothetical) proposal. On the top of one building is a plank that extends to the top of the other building. On the second building is a bag with one million dollars in it. If one of them could walk across the plank and bring the bag back, they would get to keep the million dollars. I let the idea sink in, and then I asked who was willing to do it. Typically about half or more of the hands would go up. I would then add that it's not safe, and in fact the chance of surviving the walk across the plank was only one in ten—so 90 percent of the time, the person would die. I would then, for just a moment, venture down the mathematical and statistical road with them and explain that the chance of survival was also one in ten for the walk back across, so the actual chance of surviving there and back was only one in one hundred. I would then again ask who would risk it for the million dollars. Without fail, a few of the tough guys would raise their hands and laugh.

Then I would tell them there's a new wrinkle to the situation: the plank was still there, but the money wasn't. In its place was their mother with their younger brother and sister. Also, the other building was on fire, and if their family were to survive, they would have to go over and bring them back one at a time. Who would be willing to take the risk now? Almost without fail, every hand in the auditorium would go up. That, as I explained it, was the best way I could capture and illustrate why I wanted to join the military. I wasn't doing it for money; I wasn't doing it for fame. I was doing it because I knew it was the right thing to do. I didn't understand any other way. Almost all of us recognize that we would take certain risks for the right reasons. We would risk our life to save a life, but we wouldn't necessarily take the same risk for material gain. This willingness to face risks exists because of trust. It exists in this example because the family on the other side of that plank trusts the person willing to risk his or her life to save them. The individual crossing that plank knows it's the right thing to do—they feel it in their bones and trust their own abilities to get it done.

A friend of mine and a much-loved former Blue Angel Boss in 2005–6 is Capt. Steve "Axel" Foley. Axel had a career that makes most Navy pilots want to go back and do it all over again. Over the course of almost thirty years, he never left the cockpit. He was a TOPGUN instructor not once but twice. He commanded an F/A-18 squadron and then later was the commanding officer and flight leader for the Blue Angels. As his final job in the Navy, he commanded the entire West Coast strike fighter wing—all the fighters west of the Mississippi were under his command.

Axel shared a powerful story with me that I want to share because it spoke to a level of trust that is absolutely incredible. He was selected to be the Blue Angels Boss in the spring of 2004, and he moved to NAS Pensacola in Florida that summer. In the late fall of 2004, he took command and immediately began the process of winter training. That period is a crucible for the Blue Angel team each year. As the time starts, one-third of the squadron leaves and is immediately replaced with new sailors and Marines. The process the new recruits go through to become Blue Angels takes them away from their primary job of working on the airplanes and running our squadron. At the same time, three of the six Hornet demonstration pilots are also new and go through an intense flight schedule to prepare themselves for the first air show in March. During November and December these flights are flown out of Pensacola, then the team relocates to Naval Air Facility El Centro in California for the next three months to capitalize on the great weather and excellent support out there.

Of the three new pilots each season, a new #6, the Opposing Solo, is always being trained. Generally this pilot was #7 the year before and spent that year giving backseat rides in the two-seat version of the same airplane. The profile our backseat riders fly is remarkably similar to what #6 executes during the show, and this is most definitely by design because it prepares the Opposing Solo for almost an entire year. Unfortunately, in the fall of 2004, that wasn't the case. That year's #7 was unable to remain on the team, so the individual selected to be the #7 for the following year was immediately moved up to be #6, and the team went in search of another Navy pilot to fill the role of #7. What that meant for the new #6 was that he had gotten no time at all to become comfortable in the jet, and that mattered because the Blue Angel F/A-18s were all A-model jets, meaning they were lighter and flew differently than the typical fleet Hornets.

The winter training syllabus is a building block approach that starts off with basic maneuvering that all the pilots are used to doing from their years flying Hornets off aircraft carriers. The syllabus ramps up fairly fast though, and although none of the maneuvers are necessarily new, the altitudes at which they are flown are significantly lower than the fleet standard, which is more like 10,000–30,000 feet. On flight number five, the takeoff maneuver is introduced in a simulated fashion. The takeoff maneuver normally is a low-transition, high-performance climb followed by a Split S in front of the crowd. If you're unfamiliar with what that means, it's the maneuver I described at the start of chapter 1. The Opposing Solo takes off in front of the crowd from right to left, but rather than climbing, as is traditional, he stays at the same height as if he were taxiing, just a few feet off the runway. After the aircraft reaches approximately 300 knots, he executes a maximum performance climb, establishing a 65-degree nose high climb angle. Holding that steep climb, the pilot waits until he hits 3,500 feet, then slowly rolls the aircraft on its back until it completes the top half of a loop and then continues the pull until the nose comes through the horizon. Passing the horizon the pull is continued through the vertical nose low, and then eventually he levels off the jet just in time to not hit the ground as it streaks in front of the crowd from left to right. This was the Blue Angel Opposing Solo takeoff maneuver flown every day.

Rather than having a pilot attempt this full maneuver on their very first try, we would set it up in a safer environment and simulate a takeoff from an airborne flight profile, usually 1,000–2,000 feet high and over the ocean rather than the runway. This allowed plenty of spare altitude should the maneuver not go exactly as planned. On a day during that 2004 winter, the new #6 flew it as he had rehearsed, but as he flew through the vertical portion of the loop he kept the power up and didn't increase the pull, which meant the jet's turn circle got bigger and his speed increased. Over the top of the loop this wasn't an issue, but as the jet flew through the horizon and continued nose low, the larger turn circle and higher speed meant the excess altitude wasn't going to be enough to prevent hitting the water. The pilot recognized the discrepancy through visual cues but not quite in time, and the aircraft impacted the water, portions of it actually submerged for a brief moment as the plane basically bounced off the water and continued its loop as it climbed away.

The immediate good news was it wasn't a catastrophic crash, and the pilot was not only still alive but was flying a jet that had just hit the water. Unfortunately, the jet was in pretty bad shape, and most every system that could fail was failing and fast. He immediately turned back toward the base and began executing his emergency checklists. Part of that checklist is slowing to a speed at which you can land the airplane to ensure it won't depart controlled flight and become unable to be flown. It's certainly better to determine if that's possible at high attitude when there's time to spare rather than down low when no options exist. As he performed the controllability checks it became immediately apparent that the jet couldn't slow down to a speed at which it could be landed. The decision was made to make a controlled ejection in the Gulf of Mexico and for the pilot to await being picked up by the Search and Rescue (SAR) helicopter unit. The ejection was successful, and he was subsequently plucked from the water by the SAR asset.

Meanwhile, Boss Foley was in the middle of his debrief with the diamond pilots who had just landed a few minutes before. This was also his first full week as the Boss, and he was drinking from the proverbial Blue Angel fire hose. In short, his basket was full, and he had enough on his plate in that moment simply learning how to lead the Blue Angel formation. His public affairs officer rushed into the ready room and announced, "Boss, I just got a radio call. We've got a jet in the water. We're not sure if it's 5 or 6, but we think it's 6." In time he was able to relay that it was #6, he had safely ejected, and he was being rescued by the SAR helicopter.

Boss Foley excused himself from the debrief to begin the process of managing and leading the Blue Angels through this mishap. We have a saying in the Navy: Bad news doesn't age well. And there's another in the same vein that you should never be the senior person with a secret; so Axel immediately called his boss, the Chief of Naval Air Training (CNATRA), typically a one- or two-star admiral located in Corpus Christi, Texas. He didn't have much information at that point, but he got the admiral on the phone and told him what he knew. CNATRA listened to Boss' brief and said something to the effect of "I know you'll get to the bottom of this," but more critically, what Boss Foley has never forgotten is what he said next. CNATRA simply asked, "When do you think you can get him airborne next?"

This is not just any trust; this is a profound amount of trust, and therefore confidence, in Boss Foley's leadership, in the entire Blue Angels team, and in the #6 pilot who had just crashed an airplane moments before. It's this kind of trust that breeds a level of loyalty that is hard to properly articulate. In Boss Foley's own words,

> Wow, there's another huge validation of why I'm still doing this. It's because we have the benefit of working with people like that, who didn't flinch and without knowing any details, he knew the pilot was alive and that the Blue Angels were going to figure out what went wrong and derive the right lessons from the mishap. He made that snap judgment in just three seconds and then asked when he could get him flying next.

Over the past twenty years so much has changed in our military's culture, and a story like this, viewed through the lens of naval aviation today, is shocking. Having spent that entire period flying in various squadrons both deployed and stateside, I've witnessed a gradual decline in trust and a slow and steady creep toward self-protection and career protection on the part of the commanders. Stated differently, I can't imagine any commanding officer of a squadron, an air wing, you name it, asking that as their first question. Instead, their focus would revolve around getting the proper mishap reports filed, affecting the mishap timeline, managing the guaranteed media interest, and so on. Truly and sadly, their first thoughts would likely be, *Will I be fired for this?*

I do believe the change and creep toward this has been well intentioned in a sense. There is a constant effort to reduce the number of mishaps and prevent both the loss of life and the loss of aircraft. Getting to the bottom of each mishap is critical in preventing future mishaps, and in doing so blame is placed across a wide variety of individuals and commands following each and every incident. I believe this change in our aviation culture has happened in part due to our unwillingness to tolerate mistakes, and it has had negative effects not just on naval aviation but on the military writ large. I share this story here because there's always a chance to correct and adjust. There's always an opportunity for our culture to shift back—back to a culture that trusts its leaders and its pilots and doesn't expect them to be perfect all the time. For CNATRA to make that his first concern showed an incredible confidence in all those on the Blue Angels but also in himself and even in his own boss, believing he or she would understand that he is taking the right actions to learn and move on from the mishap.

While I'm on the topic of Blue Angels, it's important to me to share a few other examples of trust that resonate and have given me a deeper understanding of how a high-performing team achieves its goals. The trust I just discussed was really the trust of leadership, and later I'll discuss the trust that existed inside our formation. But there's another layer of trust that deserves mention. A special trust exists on the Blue Angels between the pilots and their crew chiefs. Unlike all other Navy squadrons, the Blue Angels don't preflight their aircraft. Instead, they march together and climb the ladders to their jets as the ground show begins. What this means in practice is that someone else is doing the job of ensuring the jet is ready and safe for flight: the crew chief. The crew chief follows the pilot up the ladder, assists him or her with the harness and helmet, and then patiently waits while the pilot finishes the process. Many a time an observant crew chief has caught and corrected one of the pilots for a small mistake during the strap-in process. For example, if the lap belt doesn't properly buckle and latch, it would come undone at the first application of negative G. Were that to happen, it would certainly be in close formation to other jets, and if the pilot came off the seat, while inverted, it very likely would result in that aircraft being unrecoverable due to the physical inability to control the airplane.

The crew chiefs finish this process with a handshake, one of the most meaningful handshakes you'll ever receive, and a simple, "Jet's good to go, sir. Have a kickass flight." Neither the pilot nor the crew chief take that handshake lightly. The pilot has now placed total and complete trust in their crew chief.

Something often said about trust is that it's hard to earn and easy to lose. It's earned and maintained through repeated and continuous actions that are honest, open, and transparent. It's earned by keeping promises, being consistent, and demonstrating accountability. The list goes on and on. It's lost by failing in even a single one of those categories, and in my opinion, that's why trust proves to be so elusive and so incredibly valuable to a high-functioning team.

Another former Blue Angel Boss was talking to our Blue Angel team and used the term *high trust*. It immediately stayed with me to the point that I routinely use it rather than simply saying *trust*. To me, high trust means a great deal more. It means trusting someone with your life while they in turn trust you with their life—and not just once but over and over again. That's *high trust*.

A perfect Blue Angel example of high trust was made clear to me when I watched a playback of a video taken from a camera installed directly behind my head in the cockpit. In those days, camera technology wasn't as advanced or prevalent as it is now, but Boeing would visit us a few times a year and install various cameras in our airplanes so they could use the footage for their own marketing and business purposes. We would generally get a copy, and the view would be either looking back at the pilot from the front of the canopy or from overhead looking forward. I watched the air show from the camera's perspective and found it somewhat underwhelming, almost boring even, because I wasn't surprised by much—I was watching myself doing what I do every day. What did catch my eye was our final turn to land.

When I have the opportunity to speak to groups about my experiences flying Navy jets and serving on this incredibly high-functioning team, I use this as an example and play them the video. It's underwhelming in the sense that it's the top of my helmet and in the top left of the screen you can see Blue Angel #2 and, hidden behind him, Blue Angel #1. The video runs from us turning in from behind the crowd, usually at about 1,000 feet and going 250 knots, and lasts about a minute as we descend to 200 feet and accelerate to over 400 knots until we are directly over the runway and begin to execute a high-G break away to the downwind in numbered order. As you watch the video you can see the trees getting bigger, the towers passing by barely under the wingtips, even the birds go screaming by, quite surprised to see six fighters in close formation.

However, what struck me about the video was that for that entire turn, the descent to tree height, the acceleration, the close formation, never once did I look straight ahead. As pilots we're constantly taught to only look outside when we're preparing to land. We're taught to maintain that visual scan when we know our aircraft is susceptible to outside dangers and risks to flight. In this case, there were dozens of aspects that would make a pilot want to look outside and verify their flight path, altitude, speed, and such, but never once did I do so. It's simply because of that high trust. That formation, that maneuver, doesn't work unless we all maintain that same level of trust. The five wingmen are all trusting the flight leader, Blue Angel #1, to maneuver that entire formation to the perfect three-dimensional spot in space, the spot where we can safely execute our high-G turn to the downwind. We're trusting him to remain clear of the obstructions—in some cases almost threading a needle, but the thread is a formation of six F/A-18s. We're also trusting each other, as wingmen, that we *won't* look straight ahead. The airplanes are dynamic machines and are incredibly maneuverable. When you fly that close together, the number of inputs and corrections you're making with the control stick, the rudder pedals, and the throttles are so constant that it's all through learned experience and has to be second nature—there's no time to assess your deviation, think about a correction, then make the required inputs. It must happen through muscle memory. So in that environment, looking away for even a fraction of a second could result in your jet being far enough out of position to put every other member of the formation at risk. That's high trust running through that formation, powering the group, and ultimately enabling that team to be the Blue Angels.

In the previous chapter, I explained the difference in perspectives between myself, flying a low-altitude pass, and the director of *Top Gun: Maverick*, who wanted me to set up one foot to the right for the following pass. Another key aspect of that scene, and all the scenes I was a part of for the movie, was trust. Another terrific example is the scene that starts off the movie, when Maverick blasts off in the supersonic Darkstar aircraft and "dusts" the admiral who had arrived early to shut down the test flight. That scene was filmed at Naval Air Weapons Station China Lake in Ridgecrest, California, basically Death Valley. Even though most moviegoers believed it to be a fake scene or an example of computer-generated imagery (CGI), we filmed it just as you see it on the big screen. The only difference is that during editing they "reskinned" the F/A-18 I was flying so that it appeared to be the Skunk Works Darkstar instead. What they couldn't convincingly re-create with CGI was what happens to the environment and the people underneath an aircraft at low altitude, so for that reason we filmed the sequence just as it's seen. The natural risk of that type of flying with a jet at low altitude, a few mere feet over people and structures, executing a high-performance climb (HPC) is high, and we mitigated it by ensuring it was flown by someone with experience. That particular maneuver is the takeoff maneuver for Blue Angel #6, so I had already flown it thousands of times with cameras rolling and with long debriefs each time. I was confident

I could do it safely, but that doesn't mean everyone on the ground was equally confident.

The evening we filmed the scene, we had the entire Paramount crew at the end of the runway: dozens of people, trailers, cameras rolling, the whole kit and kaboodle. It was a one-shot take because the jet's exhaust was expected to cause quite a good bit of disruption to the area and the actors underneath who had just left the hair and makeup trailer. We knew from practice runs the day prior the perfect speed and location to execute the HPC, so all we had to do was add the actors and roll the cameras. As I flew overhead and performed the HPC, in addition to causing a dust storm analogous to the common Middle Eastern occurrences, it also ripped the roof off the guard shack. The dust was expected; the roof detaching most certainly was not. As luck would have it, there was some Romex wire running up the walls, through the roof and back down the other side of the building, and for that reason the roof was essentially pulled back down to its original, or approximate, location rather than ending up on top of the actors or the crew. The intensity of that scene on the ground can't be overstated, and the cinematic effect was so unbelievable that the director had to be convinced to some degree to use it because it looked fake. That's one of the aspects of *Top Gun: Maverick* I truly love: in this day and age when it's so cheap and easy to use CGI to put aerial scenes together for movies, we filmed hundreds of hours of flying to ensure what you see in that movie is real and every bit as intense as it appears. In fact, it's so real and so intense, like this HPC, that it looks fake.

Now imagine yourself at the end of the runway with an F/A-18 barreling toward you at 400–500 mph and executing an HPC just a few feet above your head. What's going through your mind? The first thing, most likely, is, *Am I going to die?* Followed shortly thereafter by, *Do I trust this guy?* Why were they all willing to stand there and risk their lives for a shot in a movie? Most of them I'd never met and might never meet. Why would they trust me in that environment? I'd submit that what they trusted were the capabilities and precision of our military and our pilots. By that point, plenty of other Navy and Marine Corps pilots had flown in various scenes, and I suspect they had a sense that the Navy was bringing in pilots who were the recognized experts in these various aspects, as I explained in chapter 2. Hopefully they recognized that I was there flying a Blue Angel airplane for that scene because I had the most experience in that flight regime and could execute it safely and with the least risk. Nonetheless, it was an incredible amount of trust they were placing in me to execute it safely.

As I stated before, trust is built up slowly over time through repeated actions, but it can be lost in an instant. A smaller crew was on location with me the day prior for our practice runs, and by executing the maneuver repeatedly at the briefed altitude, speed, and so on, I earned their trust. Imagine if on one of the many runs, I came by unexpectedly low or in a different location than we'd briefed. That one single mistake could have lost their trust and made us rethink our ability to film that scene safely.

I was introduced to the Rudyard Kipling poem "If" when I was a child. I found such meaning in it that I required all my underclassmen to memorize it when they were freshman, or Plebes, at the Naval Academy in hopes that they too would find meaning in it as I had. It has been my go-to motivation for my entire adult life when I find myself in challenging times. I will only share the first stanza because it ties in so well with this chapter, but I would encourage you each to read it in full and even commit it to memory if it resonates with you as well.

The poem begins like this:

> If you can keep your head when all about you
> Are losing theirs and blaming it on you,
> If you can trust yourself when all men doubt you,
> But make allowance for their doubting too;
> If you can wait and not be tired by waiting,
> Or being lied about, don't deal in lies,
> Or being hated, don't give way to hating,
> And yet don't look too good, nor talk too wise:

This portion can be interpreted many ways, but for me it comes down simply to trust, specifically trust in yourself. It's impossible to suffer through people blaming you, lying to you or about you, or hating you if you don't trust yourself. This is an aspect of trust I've only briefly discussed, like when I shared the example of the individual trusting themselves as they walked across the high plank to save their family. I've shared some examples about trusting your leaders, trusting your employees, and trusting those you work alongside, but not about trusting yourself. This form of trust ties into the definitions outlined earlier so clearly, and it once again comes back to confidence.

I would submit that it's impossible to fully trust yourself if you lack self-confidence. Naturally the question then is how we improve our self-confidence. What can we do to increase our trust in ourselves? I'll address this to a greater degree in a subsequent chapter about failure and how hard we have to push ourselves to be successful, but it's important to me to point out here that the most effective way to increase self-confidence is to leave your comfort zone and challenge yourself.

I often explain to people when we're discussing Blue Angel air shows that when something looks incredible from the ground, it looks absolutely surreal from inside the jet. When we have the opportunity to give backseat rides to fellow F/A-18 pilots, many who've spent their careers flying these exact planes, they are often speechless. Those maneuvers, though, don't happen that way the first time we practice them—quite the opposite, in fact. We slowly and methodically reduce the separation, increase the closure, and so on until we have a finished product we're proud of. Doing that, though, requires each of the pilots to get outside of their comfort zone—pushing themselves, challenging themselves even when it's not natural and certainly not comfortable.

That has so many corollaries in other endeavors. Regardless of your pursuit, whether it be at work or in your personal life, if you want to achieve a greater degree of self-confidence, if you want to increase your trust in yourself, you must push your own bounds and test your limits because you won't know what they are until you do that. It takes setting goals and working toward them, regardless of whether it's comfortable or easy.

It's when you begin to see your confidence improve and begin to trust yourself more that you find you can keep a level head when all around you are losing theirs and trust yourself when all others doubt you.

I learned how to be a Blue Angel pilot flying on the wing of one of the most incredible people I've ever met: then-Major Nate "Corky" Miller, USMC. In a business full of big personalities and impressive people, Corky is in a league all his own. He's a talented pilot, but more importantly, he's one of the most genuine and passionate people I've ever met, and he exudes passion with everything he says and does. When I joined the Blue Angels, he was finishing up his year as #7, the narrator and VIP pilot, and moving into the role of the Opposing Solo pilot. As such, he became my de facto mentor and guided me along my first year as #7 and then was my flight lead when he moved up to #5, our Lead Solo position, and I became the Opposing Solo.

There's so much risk involved in each job on the Blue Angels, but our #6 pilots have a mishap rate that's significantly greater than the rest of the pilots. I've already alluded to one of them, and I'll share more stories in subsequent chapters as well. Needless to say, the job of Lead Solo carries with it a great deal of responsibility to ensure you properly train your wingman. Corky did that for me better than anyone else could have ever done. He was meticulous in how he briefed each new maneuver; he was laser-focused when we were in the air to evaluate everything I did and then brought it back to our debrief so I could learn. He invested himself into my training in a way I had never seen before.

Having someone like that teaching me made it a lot easier the first time we pointed our jets at one another to introduce our opposing passes. The bread and butter of the Solo portion of the Blue Angel air shows is our timing pattern that gets us to a point where we can cross in front of the crowd mere feet apart with over 1,000 mph of closure. With that amount of relative closure, our jets were converging and covering 1,667 feet every second. At that speed and closure rate, there's very little room for error, and the level of trust in each other is paramount. The Lead Solo flies a prebriefed line over the ground, typically along a runway edge or show line, while the Opposing Solo crosses at a separation based on their experience, proficiency, and the environments. The ability to converge closer and closer with each successive pass comes through the building of trust between the two pilots. It takes repeated, continuous events to build that trust, and a single mistake can have devastating consequences.

Trust is the engine that powers high-performing teams. Any other characteristic that might do the job can't fully exist or function without trust. That trust exists because it's earned and maintained. The trust on high-functioning teams almost always exists because it starts at the top. It starts with honor and transparency. It is built further by a willingness to be vulnerable and to be self-aware enough to change and adapt. Perhaps the most wonderful aspect of trust is that it's a virtuous cycle. When one acts in such a way to earn the trust of others and, at the same time, trusts them, it becomes contagious in such a way that it multiplies among the rest of the team. It is, in my opinion, the single most critical aspect of teamwork.

Note

1 *Merriam-Webster Dictionary*, s.v. "trust," accessed 19 December 2024, https://www.merriam-webster.com/dictionary/trust.

Lt. (jg) Benjamin Becker (*left*) and Lt. (jg) Frank Weisser at the winging ceremony at NAS Meridian, November 2002 *Photo credit unknown*

VFA-87 (Strike Fighter Squadron 87) "War Party" at sea, deployed on the USS *Theodore Roosevelt*, receiving the Top Hook award for landing performance while deployed from August 2005 to February 2006. *Photo credit unknown*

Lt. Frank Weisser presents filmmaker Brian Terwilliger with a lithograph following a VIP flight in the back seat of Blue Angel #7 on 19 February 2008. *Photo credit unknown*

Lt. Frank Weisser, the Blue Angels #7 pilot, signs autographs after a Blue Angels demonstration at the Barksdale Air Force Base air show in Bossier City, Louisiana, on 10 May 2008. *U.S. Navy photo by MC1 Kimberly R. Stephens (Released) 080510-N-8390S-376 BOSSIER CITY, LA*

Lt. Frank Weisser preparing to strap in with the help of his crew chief, Aviation Structural Mechanic Petty Officer 1st Class (AM1) Cory Keller, in 2009. *Photo credit unknown*

Lt. Frank Weisser performs the Blue Angel #6 low-transition takeoff maneuver during the Marine Corps Air Station Miramar air show in October 2009. *Photo credit unknown*

Blue Angel Delta Formation pilots in 2009. From left: Cdr. Greg McWherter, Lt. Cdr. Paul Brantuas, Maj. Christopher Collins, Lt. Mark Swinger, Maj. Nate Miller, Lt. Frank Weisser *Photo credit unknown*

VFA-97 (Strike Fighter Squadron 97) "Warhawks" at sea, deployed on the USS *John C. Stennis* during a combat deployment, 2012–13 *Photo credit unknown*

Lt. Cdr. Frank Weisser meets his daughter Caroline for the first time following an eight-month combat deployment, 28 April 2013. *Photo credit unknown*

Cdr. Frank Weisser shown taxiing for an air show with the Blue Angels, 20 May 2017. *U.S. Navy photo by PO2 Ian Cotter*

Cdr. Frank Weisser, Lead Solo pilot for the Blue Angels in 2017, is shown flying in formation. *Glen Watson*

The Blue Angels Fleur-de-Lis maneuver, 16 October 2005 *Photo credit unknown*

Cdr. Frank Weisser is being strapped into the *Top Gun: Maverick* F/A-18E Super Hornet (BUNO 165536) with the help of his crew chief, Aviation Ordnanceman Petty Officer 2nd Class (AO2) Aldriick Kittles. *Capt. Scott Janik*

Airborne in the *Top Gun: Maverick* jet, 14 June 2019 *Photo credit: Cdr. Frank Weisser*

Practice runs at Naval Air Warfare Center Weapons Division China Lake for the *Top Gun: Maverick* Darkstar Takeoff Scene, 8 November 2018 *Photo credit unknown*

Camera crew selfie during the extreme low-altitude flyover in *Top Gun: Maverick*, 14 May 2019 *Photo credit unknown*

Cdr. Frank Weisser is shown flying the extreme low-altitude flyover in *Top Gun: Maverick*, 16 May 2019. *Photo credit unknown*

CHAPTER 4

COMMUNICATION

"Be your own biggest critic. Don't let someone else beat you to constructive criticism."

—CHRISTINA TOSI

Blue Angel #1 (Boss):	"Ease the pull, rolling out the Fleur-de-Lis, a little drive."
#2:	"Zesty"
#3:	"Indy"
#4:	"Kitty"
#5:	"Walleye"
#6:	"Baxter"
Boss:	"Up we go."
Boss:	"Smoke on."
Boss:	"Ready break."

THOSE FEW SECONDS of airborne inter-cockpit communication prepare, initiate, and execute the Blue Angels' Fleur-de-Lis maneuver. That maneuver is one of if not my absolute favorite Blue Angel maneuvers. Despite the good-natured teasing that exists between the two airborne elements of the

Blue Angels, the Diamond and the Solos, the teamwork displayed for the last portion of the show, when all six aircraft join up together, is what really accentuates the excellence of the Blue Angels.

When they have finished maneuvering the individual elements, the six planes join up into one unit called the Delta formation. In this formation the Diamond remains intact—with #2 on the right wing, #3 on the left wing, and #4, the Slot pilot, directly below and behind the #1 jet—and #5 joins on the left side, off the wing of #3, and #6 joins on the right side of the formation, outboard of #2. This Delta formation can now demonstrate the Blue Angels' precision capabilities while incorporating several dynamic high-G maneuvers and a few crossing maneuvers.

The Fleur-de-Lis has it all. It follows the Delta Roll, a maneuver where all six aircraft gracefully roll 360 degrees as one unit above the crowd. After the Delta Roll, the jets shift their formation slightly with #5 and #6 shifting inboard and flying directly under the left and right wingman, making the formation taller but narrower and, more important, allowing for the dynamic maneuvering that takes place next. What allows all this to take place in the air is as basic as it is challenging, and it's done through simple airborne communications. As the Boss rolls out the formation left of the crowd on the show line, he depresses the button for the Delta frequency, the radio channel to which all six pilots as well as the support personnel on the ground are now dialed. After keying the mic (aviation parlance for depressing the comm switch), he says, "Ease the pull, rolling out the Fleur-de-Lis, a little drive." Every word of that matters, as does the rate at which it's said and its intensity.

Our comms allow us to do what we do in the sky—and, more importantly, do it safely. Through the comms, the flight lead can change any maneuver by adjusting his words, their speed, and their intensity.

The phrase "ease the pull" means just what it sounds like. On this maneuver, all the pilots have aft stick inputs, meaning they're each individually pulling back on their control sticks a small amount to keep their jets in a left-hand turn in the proper positions in the formation. When Boss says, "ease the pull," they each slightly relax their control stick, which in turn slows the rate of the overall turn and allows for a smoother eventual rollout. The most important aspect, considering how closely these six highly maneuverable jets are flying in formation, is how much they ease the pull. That amount is learned through hundreds of hours of training while the flight lead stays incredibly consistent with his comms and his maneuvering. Hundreds of repetitions of this maneuver are flown, videoed, and debriefed during the Blue Angels' winter training period. Doing so allows each pilot to see how their flying and their control inputs compared to what Boss and the other jets did and then subsequently to make slight adjustments until all the aircraft stay in their positions throughout the turn and rollout.

If Boss noticed the wind was pushing the formation more than expected and the rollout was going to be late, he would simply increase the speed with which he said those words. Hearing a faster tempo would immediately alert the other pilots that their normal control inputs would need to be faster. How much faster is proportionate to the speed of the comms. That's the genius behind using comms to drive the formation. The Boss can at any time adjust the established, practiced maneuvers with just the words and the way in which he says them.

The comms must at all times stay clear and concise. This critical aspect of communications is not unique to the Blue Angels; it is paramount for all aviation, and we address it daily, if not constantly, in naval aviation. It's a common mantra heard from instructors as students go through their training, and it extends all the way to our most advanced school, TOPGUN, where our most capable pilots train to be even more lethal in the jet. Because any communication in aviation can either aid or harm what is happening, the comms must be clear. It is imperative that aviators and anyone else involved, namely the controllers, use clear communications, whether it's the tower controllers, the approach controllers, or the airborne interdiction controllers. Clear communications are never more critical than when airborne, where simple mistakes and miscommunications can be fatal.

There is an incredible amount of communication required to maneuver the Blue Angels' Delta formation around, and that's when everything is going smoothly. A perfect example of the necessity of clear and concise communications comes from one of the very few annual air shows the Blue Angels fly in Seattle, Washington, known as Seafair. The air show is flown over Lake Washington—an incredible location for an air show. Seattle's primary airport is Seattle-Tacoma International Airport (SeaTac), which is an extremely busy airfield. Throughout the entirety of the air show, large commercial aircraft are taking off to the north and executing an almost immediate left turn to not "penetrate the bubble" of the air show airspace. At the same time, Blue Angel maneuvers and rendezvous routinely take place 4.5–5.0 nm behind the crowd, which is at the outer edges of the airspace (5 nm radius), and a spillover or spill-out of even a tenth of a mile (less than 1 second of travel) could lead to an unintended deconfliction issue. This aspect alone keeps all the pilots, both those taking off from SeaTac and the Blue Angel pilots, very much focused on the elevated level of risk and minimal room for error.

Once again, that's when everything is going smoothly. This story is about what happened when a small aircraft, sightseeing around beautiful Seattle, ended up in the middle of the air show. Although the information is published well in advance and made available to pilots on a variety of charts and planning apps, it's not abnormal for an "interloper" to find themselves in the air show airspace. When this happens, the intrusion can be communicated in a variety of ways. Sometimes the tower sees it on radar and passes it to the Blue Angels' representative stationed in the tower, who then radios it to their representative at the communications cart, who then notifies the pilots in the air. Sometimes this game of telephone can be strung out and/or miscommunicated due to the rate of travel of the various aircraft.

During this particular year at the Seafair show we were flying our typical air show, albeit in challenging airspace as previously mentioned, when an interloper entered the air show airspace, also referred to as a TFR or Temporary Flight Restriction due to the Federal Aviation Administration (FAA) effectively closing off this airspace because of the show. Without a moment's hesitation our maintenance officer, who was running the comm cart, transmitted on our frequency: "Interloper 3 miles in front of the crowd,

crowd left [our abbreviation for its position relative to center point], 1,000 feet heading west." There was no possible way to state the aircraft's position and track any clearer or more concisely than he did in that moment, and it allowed all the pilots to locate and deconflict from the unknown aircraft immediately.

A remarkable aspect of the Blue Angels is that the primary focus and mission for the team is the airborne demonstration. As such, every member of the team has a job related to the demonstration, and our support officers train to do jobs they've never done before. For example, our maintenance officer (MO) runs the comm cart, which is composed of almost a dozen people. The MO is accompanied by our flight surgeon (Doc), who grades the demonstration and functions as a safety observer. Both of those individuals can key their mics and talk to the pilots at any time. They are accompanied by another Blue Angels officer, who acts as a liaison to the tower, along with multiple other Blue Angels enlisted team members, some of whom act as liaisons with the maintenance department and others who video the demonstration for debrief and safety purposes. None of these individuals had any prior experience or training talking on a radio in an aviation environment, yet they all had to learn the skills of clear and concise communication because of the critical nature of our demonstration. Doing the jobs well requires a high level of situational awareness—that is, knowing where all the airplanes are at all times, even when they can't be seen, by listening to the constant comm chatter and by watching the show so many times that the ground tracks become memorized. In that moment in Seattle, the quick reaction of our MO, Sam

Rose, along with his absolutely perfect comm, likely saved the jets from a disastrous situation.

As mentioned previously, in addition to being clear, good comms are concise, meaning expressing or covering much in few words—brief in form but comprehensive in scope. Whether it's a Blue Angels demonstration with six pilots communicating constantly both inside the formation and back and forth with a communications cart or it's a fifty-plus plane exercise in the ranges outside of TOPGUN at NAS Fallon (NV), concise comms is not just a priority; it's an imperative.

Nearly every aspect of aviation communication is intended to be concise—as the definition expresses, how can we communicate the most information in the fewest words? That's true from the most basic comms required for taxi, takeoff, and check-in with departure controllers all the way to check-in with the AIC (Airborne Intercept Controller). Each word said on the radio between the pilots and controllers is designed, practiced, and executed to be brief in form but comprehensive in scope.

NAS Fallon, home of TOPGUN and Strike, is where all carrier air wings go to train before their deployments. The training cycle includes a buildup starting with small exercises designed with sections of airplanes—that is, two jets, one as the flight lead and the other as the wingman. These flights include both the prosecuting of airborne threats from long distances away through dogfighting training and dropping ordnance on ground targets. After moving through these more basic training exercises, the number of airplanes and the complexity of the missions increase substantially. The "graduation" exercises generally comprise large groups of airplanes, with twenty to thirty jets, flying as they would for a large-force strike against dozens of other jets simulating enemy aircraft along with ground stations. In addition to all these airborne assets, multiple other controllers on the ground assist both the good guys and the bad guys. On the good guys' side, the easiest job is possibly the fighters who are primarily listening to two radio frequencies—the first being the primary frequency everyone listens to and communicates on, the second being a subset of that group, perhaps just the aircraft assigned to prosecute enemy fighters. A group of jets behind them are the attackers who are loaded with ordnance to strike a ground target. They're on the same primary frequency, but they're also on a secondary frequency with the other strikers. Our airborne controllers have even more complicated comms because they are on the primary frequency directing the fighters toward the enemy aircraft, on a secondary frequency communicating internally with the other two controllers in the back of their E-2 Hawkeye, and on yet another frequency communicating with their two pilots who are in the front of the formation to help them maneuver to keep the best coverage. They might also be monitoring other frequencies with ground controllers to ensure they're aware of any safety concerns or interlopers in the area.

The communication aspect of a large-force exercise is complicated, intense, and dynamic. Being adept at communicating concisely is a necessary skill, and the pilots and controllers who can communicate information that is comprehensive in scope but brief in form separates the good from the great.

For the Blue Angels' Fleur-de-Lis maneuver, the comms must be exceedingly clear and concise. Once the pull has been eased, the next communication is "rolling out, the Fleur-de-Lis"; and much like the preceding comm, these words matter a great deal. The phrase "rolling out" is the preparatory command, while "the" is the command of execution, meaning as "the" is said, all six pilots take out the left stick inputs, causing their aircraft to turn left, and then they center the sticks, allowing them to fly straight and level in their current formation. "A little drive" is very much Blue Angel specific, and it tells the pilots to push forward slightly on the stick, causing the jets to descend a minute amount. Because of the spring on the stick, there's really very little pushing required; in fact, it's more of an ease to allow the stick to travel slightly forward and get the jets moving closer to the ground while staying in formation.

As soon as the Boss finishes that first line of comms, the five other pilots acknowledge ("ack") the comm with their individual call signs. This gives the Boss and each of the wingmen confidence that they heard the call and are prepared for the maneuver. This happens dozens of times over the course of the demonstration.

"Up we go" comes next, usually when the jets are just over 2 nm at crowd left. That distance is a bit farther than you might first imagine, and it demonstrates just how fast the jets are traveling because they will cover those 2 miles in under 20 seconds. Starting that far to the left ensures the maneuver will happen directly in front of the crowd. That comm gets all the jets to begin their climb. "Up we" is the preparatory command, and "go" is the command of execution. On the *g* of "go," all six pilots pull back on their sticks.

However, what's most critical is not that they're just pulling back on their sticks at the same time. It's that they are pulling back at the same time, to the same degree, and with the same rate of change. All those aspects are absolutely critical and are required, like all the rest, for the safe execution of this maneuver.

If one of the pilots pulled back at the correct time but didn't pull back quite as much as the other five, that jet would have a shallower climb gradient and its position inside the formation, relative to the other jets, would change almost instantaneously. Because the aircraft are just feet apart, that distance of safe separation can disappear in less than a second, so the displacement of the stick is critical. Likewise, the rate of change matters just as much. The acceleration of each jet into the vertical also has the same ability to alter the placement of each jet and therefore the overall formation. Thus, this entire dynamic movement of jets in close formation is dependent on well-rehearsed, clear, concise communication and is built on the trust that the other pilots will be equally focused and attuned to the comms.

The closest analogy I can provide for those not in the business of flying Blue Angels air shows is to picture yourself at a traffic light, waiting patiently in line for the light to change from red to green. As the light turns green, the first in line takes their foot off the brake and places it on the gas and begins to accelerate. The car behind allows what they deem to be safe separation to build, then does the exact same thing. As they accelerate, they naturally end up farther behind the car than they were at the light. This progression continues down the line of cars waiting at the light so that, ultimately, the cars that originally had only a few feet between them now have hundreds of feet between them. In doing so, there is a bit of an accordion effect that builds. That accordion effect is what the Blue Angels work so hard at to avoid. If it were merely a game of follow the leader, the formation would be dictated by each pilot's individual reaction time along with a variety of other challenges. The formations would vary and change so much over the course of an air show that it's unlikely anyone would be impressed. In an effort to keep our jets in their correct positions throughout the entire show, we use those very specific comms.

For the Fleur-de-Lis, the maneuver isn't over at the roll-out or the initial climb; in fact, it is just beginning. At 7 degrees nose high, Boss says, "Smoke on," and with that comm each pilot actuates their smoke using a switch on their throttle. Pulling the switch aft releases the smoke oil that resides in a tank in the nose of the jet (a space normally occupied by a 20-mm cannon), which then travels through piping running the entire length of the jet and is expelled into the air directly behind and above the left engine. The hot air from the exhaust then converts the smoke oil into the white billowy smoke that has become such a recognizable part of the Blue Angels shows.

Just a second or two later, with the jets now 15 degrees nose high, Boss keys the mic and says, "Ready break," and the *k* in "break" is the command of execution. The instant that *k* is transmitted, all six aircraft break apart in a very dramatic manner. The Boss pulls 4 Gs into the vertical, the left and right wingmen each pull 2.5 Gs away from the formation, and the slot pilot holds the exact same flight path. Underneath the slot pilot, the two solo pilots each roll away from the formation with a 45-degree bank angle while also simultaneously pushing 2 negative Gs. This creates an almost intermediate separation between the six jets. Just one second after the "Ready break" comm from Boss, once #4 sees safe separation he makes the call "Ready roll," thereby commanding all pilots to roll their aircrafts. Blue Angels #5 and #6 each roll their jets one and a half times, or 540 degrees, to end up in an inverted flight attitude, while the four diamond pilots each execute an aileron roll of 360 degrees and then proceed to effect an extremely fast and dynamic rendezvous on the lead jet in the vertical while Boss completes a looping maneuver.

Meanwhile the two Solo pilots, having extended straight ahead in an inverted position, roll their jets 270 degrees and commence a 7+ G turn behind the crowd to rendezvous with each other prior to rejoining the Diamond. This part of the demonstration is undeniably one of the most dynamic and challenging portions of the entire show for the two Solo pilots. There is a great deal of concentration and focus that takes place throughout the Delta Roll and into the start of the Fleur-de-Lis. The position-keeping alone is challenging, not to mention the multitude of procedures taking place in a very short time frame. Being mentally task-saturated is a common danger to high-G maneuvering because it's easy to forget the critical requirement of the anti-G straining maneuver (AGSM) when your brain is focused on flying the right formation, saying the right thing at the right time, actuating the smoke at the correct instant, breaking apart from the formation at the right angle of bank and proper negative G, then completing the correct number of rolls in the correct direction, and on it goes. If the pilot's focus is too weighted on those procedures, when the rollout happens behind the crowd and the high-G turn is commenced, the magnitude of the G in that turn can quickly, if not almost instantly, result in G-induced loss of consciousness (G-LOC) of the pilot.

Unknown to most spectators but *very* relevant to the pilots is the fact that G-suits are not used by the Blue Angels. G-suits are chaps for pilots. They strap and zip up around the pilot's legs and abdomen and are connected to the jet with a hose to allow the jet to fill the G-suit with air when it's placed under positive G forces. The higher the G, the more air the jet forces into the suit, and the G-suit then functionally squeezes the pilot's legs and abdomen in an attempt to prevent the blood from leaving the pilot's head and pooling in their lower extremities due to the G forces pulling the blood down. G-suits have proven extremely effective over the years and are an indispensable part of any fighter jet.

There are two critical reasons why the Blue Angels don't wear G-suits when they fly. The first and more important reason is that the airplane is flown with the rudder pedals shifted aft so the pilot's feet are much closer to their body than the normal position. This shift allows the pilots to comfortably rest their right forearm on their right thigh to help mitigate the effect and stress of the spring on the stick. Resting the stick-arm on their thigh also allows for the high degree of control that is required for the precision formation flying that is synonymous with the Blue Angels. Were they to wear a G-suit the air bladders on their legs would inflate under G, thereby lifting their right forearm and causing unintended inputs to the controls and thus altering the formation. The second reason relates to the air bladder that covers the abdomen. The Blue Angel harness is slightly modified from a fleet jet's harness in that it adds a lap belt, which is cinched down extremely tight to remove any possibility of body shifts when flying inverted. Because of the positioning of the lap belt, the G-suit portion that covers that abdomen would be useless and moreover might cause functional problems with the belt and its connection point.

Those aspects combine to render the Blue Angels unable to use a G-suit, and so more attention and respect must be paid to the capabilities of the jet and the pilots are absolutely required to be "ahead of the G." It's very manageable; but much like the rest of their flying, an honest mistake can be followed by a harsh punishment.

The Solo pilots complete their rendezvous behind the crowd, then fly a formation barrel roll in front of the crowd while rendezvousing with the Diamond for their next maneuver, the Loop Break Cross. I highlight this particular maneuver, the Fleur-de-Lis, because it combines all that is great about the Blue Angels. It's precise formation flying, dynamic maneuverability of the jets, multiple breakups and rejoins (which are almost always the most challenging portions of the demonstration), and display of teamwork from the Delta formation and the entire Blue Angel team are what are required to fly this portion of the show.

That being said, all the clear and concise communication aside, two other aspects of communication are what truly set the Blue Angels apart and what allow them to function at such a high level: the communication that happens once the show is over. First, after the jets land, the pilots quickly debrief the maintenance department on any issues they noticed with their planes, and then immediately head to the crowd line to visit with the spectators. The time at the crowd line is certainly the most valuable portion of the Blue Angels' mission, and it's what I love most about the team.

The air show and the demonstration of their skills give the Blue Angels the credibility to have these conversations with the spectators, specifically the children and the young men and women who have watched the show. The critical point here is that the pilots aren't there to talk about the show and explain what it's like to fly loops to Van Halen songs; they're using the air show to tell the really important stories—the ones about the men and women deployed abroad and in harm's way.

If the pilots didn't do a show and instead just walked around talking to the crowd, they wouldn't necessarily generate much interest or have a significant impact on any of the spectators. Despite the nearly skin-tight, bright blue flight suits, the Blue Angels need the air show to have the opportunity to make those connections with the attendees. Watching a Blue Angels air show is much more than just watching airplanes fly. The power and sound from the jets make it a full-body experience; watching a video of it will never compare to being there in person and covering your ears from the noise of the engines in afterburner or feeling your insides almost move as the jets scream by overhead. This experience has no real equal, so when young men and women experience the demonstration, then watch the airplanes land, taxi directly in front of them, and shut down, their eyes are naturally drawn to the pilots as they unstrap and dismount from their jets. When these same pilots then come straight to them, it can be an overwhelming experience for some of them, having a chance to ask questions and make a direct human connection with the show they just watched.

This sort of thing doesn't generally happen at other events or shows. When a movie ends, the actors don't appear out of the screen and approach the moviegoers. At the end of a concert, following the applause and bows, the musicians don't wander into the crowd to mingle—that's generally reserved for the very few who have backstage access. At the end of a sporting event, it's rare to see a player, much less have them approach the fans and spend half an hour to an hour talking, answering questions, taking pictures, and so on. So we truly believe this time in our day is some of the most important for achieving our mission; in fact, it's our final piece of the puzzle.

That time is not meant to be used for trying to enlist the young men and women into the military but rather to share what we each love about our jobs and about aviation. This time separates good Blue Angels from great Blue Angels. When we choose our team members, for the pilots, the flying aspect is critical. Many men and women who fly Navy jets have the ability to fly our air show, especially given how much time we allow ourselves for training. What truly separates those we hire from the rest is how they're able to effectively share their love for service, for naval aviation, and for aviation in general. Those who truly love what they do are often best suited to share it with others.

I found many times that the applicants who desperately wanted to be a Blue Angel or, worse, had wanted to be a Blue Angel their entire life didn't necessarily make great teammates. Why they weren't always great Blue Angels wasn't intuitive for me at first. The fact of the matter is that every job in the military starts with service and putting the needs of our country, and in our case the needs of the Navy, ahead of ourselves. Those who chose to serve because they felt called to do so, rather than because they were convinced for any variety of reasons, seemed to be better able to selflessly give. Those who wanted to be a Blue Angel in order to share their love for their country and for aviation always, in my opinion, seemed to be more successful in furthering our mission than those who made it about themselves.

I share this thought because it speaks to other aspects of our lives, and it certainly extends beyond Blue Angels air shows. I firmly believe that when you give, you get more than you take, at a very basic level. It's always more fun to give a present and watch the joy of someone receiving it than to get a gift. My twenty-five years in the military were rewarding in so many ways, but the opportunity to give and to serve was chief among them. There is a quiet satisfaction that comes from serving others, and I believe that satisfaction allows us all to be better, more well-balanced individuals. I've told my sailors over the years that we're all serving and being served throughout our lives, but if we can focus on the serving part and not the being served, we'll be more grateful in general and also better custodians of the positions we find ourselves in. Those who joined the Blue Angels to serve those around them were certainly better at our mission than those who joined simply for the achievement and distinction of being a Blue Angel.

This also speaks to the concept that communication doesn't have to be written or spoken. We communicate very powerfully through our actions, and the action of service is exceptionally formidable as a communication tool. I believe those who serve others are easily recognizable and are afforded an increased level of respect because of their decision to serve rather than be served. Whether it's a healthcare worker, a police officer, or a teacher, they're immediately respected because of their choice to serve, which is communicated through their actions, not their words.

When I had those opportunities to be at the crowd line with young and old alike, it was always important to me to use the time to share the really important story and the real reason we were there, which was simply that at the exact moment we stood there having just finished our air show, my military brothers and sisters were working on the flight deck and flying off the aircraft carrier into harm's way in the dark of night. I would share with them that we don't have the ability to take every person aboard our aircraft carriers, and we certainly couldn't allow them to see flight operations while at sea, but if they could witness it, they'd never think of aviation or being at sea the same again.

I distinctly remember the first time I ever saw the flight deck of an aircraft carrier, and it was fifteen seconds before I landed on it for the first time ever. Despite having attended the Naval Academy and having been flying Navy jets for two years, the first time I ever saw a flight deck was when I rolled out into the groove (our term for the straightaway portion directly behind the aircraft carrier landing area) and had the last fifteen seconds of my approach to make sense of this enormous ship at sea onto which it was somehow possible to land a fighter jet. The closest I ever came prior to that was during a Midshipman Cruise the summer before my junior year at the Naval

Academy. All the Midshipmen at the Academy spend their summers doing training to better prepare themselves for being commissioned and taking over in their respective roles, whether that be in a squadron, a ship, a submarine, or elsewhere. That particular summer I was assigned to the USS *Vincennes*, CG-49, a guided-missile cruiser stationed in Yokuska, Japan. The Navy's cruisers are massive ships; ours was 567 feet in length, displaced almost 10,000 tons, and required a crew of 330 sailors and officers to operate. We happened to be docked next to the USS *Independence* (CV 62) and despite it being slightly smaller than the more typical *Nimitz*-class carriers, it was still incredibly big. They wouldn't let me aboard, so I tried to see the flight deck by climbing as high as I could on my ship. Despite getting to the highest point I could reach, climbing multiple ladders all the way up to the radar dishes onboard the *Vincennes*, I still wasn't anywhere near the height of the flight deck, which sits roughly 60 feet above the waterline.

So having landed aboard the aircraft carrier for the very first time, I did what almost everyone does on their first landing: I sat there paralyzed, convinced I'd just crashed, staring straight ahead. I had full power selected with my left hand, out of muscle memory from hundreds of practice landings, until I noticed sailors jumping up and down in front of my jet giving me the signal to power back and raise my hook so I could get out of the landing area (LA) in time for the next student to land. It was only after I'd taxied out of the LA and hooked up to a refueling hose that I was able to begin to process what I'd just done and where I was. I was onboard the USS *John F. Kennedy* and about 100 miles off the coast of its homeport in Jacksonville, Florida, while the 100,000-ton carrier steamed into the wind for the other student pilots to land. As I sat in the cockpit of my T-45C Goshawk, having slightly come down off the high of landing on a carrier for the first time, I realized that the vessel I was on was literally a floating city and men and women were running in nearly every direction, knowing precisely what they were doing. I remember thinking if only they knew how totally clueless I was in that very moment, they might not be so cavalier and would instead keep a safe distance from me.

During that short period before I taxied to the catapult for my first aircraft carrier launch and then downwind for more landings, I distinctly remember having a sense of excitement for my career. In that moment I wanted nothing more than to spend my career flying off aircraft carriers; I was completely overwhelmed by the environment and experience. Our challenge, in fact our charter to some degree, on the Blue Angels is to share that sentiment, to make that experience come to life through our communication. If we can tell the story properly, if we can bring that experience to life, it's a powerful message to share with everyone, from young men and women all the way to the Greatest Generation of our veterans. Just recounting some of these stories and experiences can bring them back to life, and you can see a twinkle in the eye of a World War II or Vietnam-era pilot as they flash back for a moment to some of the most exciting periods of their life. When you communicate it properly to our youth, it can do far more; it might very likely redirect the course of their life and set them on a path to serving their country in a similar manner.

The message and story I tried my best to communicate after an air show was just how incredible it was to be able not just to live on but to operate airplanes off a ship at sea and that it was far more incredible than the air show they'd just watched. However, since we cannot bring each and every person in our great nation out to an aircraft carrier, we try to bring a slice of naval aviation to them by flying our show. The demonstration shows takeoff and landing maneuvers, it shows the aircraft flying with its landing gear and tailhooks down, and it tries to demonstrate the various capabilities of our aircraft that allow it to be both a fighter and an attack jet along with being able to land aboard a ship at sea.

Our air show is sometimes most effective when we fly in small towns that are nowhere near an ocean and have no Navy presence within hundreds, if not thousands, of miles. Those shows can have the most positive effect for us as we showcase the Navy and Marine Corps pride and professionalism with the help of our awesome jets and our incredible sailors and Marines. These are the shows that change the trajectory of young men's and women's lives.

This was the case for my first ever roommate. On day one at the Naval Academy in the summer of 1996, I was introduced to Benjamin J. Becker from Idaho Falls, Idaho. Ben came to the Naval Academy from a relatively small town in eastern Idaho. He'd found out somewhat late that he was accepted, and his plan was to fly jets. He was very athletic and had been a star high school basketball player. He was also a somewhat accomplished pilot, having already gotten his license while in high school, and he was very much not prepared for the military experience. He had an absolute heart of gold, but spending the next six weeks being yelled at and run ragged wasn't exactly how he'd expected to be prepared to be a fighter pilot. Nonetheless, once he settled into his rhythm, Ben excelled in all aspects of being a midshipman. More important Ben made an impact on the students and staff far and wide in Annapolis.

In addition to being a hopeless romantic, having flown his high school sweetheart all over eastern Idaho and spending entirely too much time thinking of how he would convince her to marry a Navy pilot, he was a kind and generous soul. All the students at the Naval Academy received a "Career Starter Loan" of $22,000 at little to no interest. The loan was generally used to buy a car or get established with the bare necessities that are required when leaving a four-year military school and transitioning to living in the real world. Ben spent the lion's share of his loan flying his entire extended family to Annapolis for graduation week. He bought nearly thirty airplane tickets for his immediate family, grandparents, aunts, uncles, and cousins. He set them up in hotel rooms and got them tickets to meet their representative in Washington, D.C., tour the Capitol, go to an amusement park, and more. Very few of them had ever been on an airplane before, much less left Idaho because they were a family of farmers and rarely could get away. In fact, that year they changed the schedule for the annual cattle drive to allow them all to spend the week away.

When Ben sent them his graduation announcement, he included in each envelope the printed airline tickets and the itinerary for the week, and at the bottom he wrote, "Please don't bring a gift. Your presence is your present." He told me he wasn't sure they could each afford to buy him a graduation present, and he knew that just leaving their farms was a huge sacrifice they each had to make. I joined him to pick them up at the BWI (Baltimore/Washington International Thurgood Marshall Airport), and the smile on his face was perhaps the greatest I'd ever seen. He was so excited and proud to have his family there and I just couldn't get over his level of generosity and love for family.

Ben made an impact for years to come and flew multiple deployments around the world as a C-2A Greyhound pilot. Ben was tragically killed in an airplane accident in the summer of 2005, along with his father, Bill, and brother, Andy. At their funeral the church overflowed with people, with many more waiting outside. Ben's entire squadron of pilots, officers, and sailors flew to Idaho from San Diego to attend and support Ben's mother and sister. The fighter pilots from Ben's most recent deployment did a missing-man flyover as his grandfather on horseback pulled their family wagon loaded down under the weight of three caskets. It was the most moving ceremony I have ever witnessed.

Ben joined the military because as a young man he saw the Blue Angels perform in Idaho Falls. That day's air show changed the trajectory of his life, and in doing so, it also changed the lives of hundreds, maybe even thousands, of midshipmen, sailors, and friends who got to know Ben Becker. My constant refrain to myself while I flew air shows all over our country was that if I could just find one more Ben Becker, inspire one young man or young woman who might have a similar impact, then I would have more than fulfilled my mission as a Blue Angel. Ben was the best man I ever met—no one else comes close.

The communication that takes place at the crowd line is critical. It is our chance to share with young and old our love for naval aviation and our genuine excitement to serve our country. It's also the time to remind each of them that we're just pilots flying in perfect weather surrounded by cheering spectators and that the ones we are cheering are the men and women who in that very moment are flying off aircraft carriers at night into enemy territory. They don't receive any cheers, yet their flying is unquestionably the most dangerous and most challenging the Navy does. I love that the Blue Angels air show gave us the platform not to talk about ourselves, but to tell the important stories and to make sure our public knew it was happening. As I say this, it's important to note that in this very moment we have men and women working in the most dangerous environment in the world: the flight deck of an aircraft carrier at night. Our carriers are constantly deployed around the world, so in this very moment our sailors are serving, in the dark, off the coast of hostile areas to ensure our freedom and democracy remain in place. They're doing it this precise moment.

What makes the Blue Angels a high-functioning team is actually what transpires after they depart the crowd line. The team rejoins in their briefing space, which varies from airport to airport but is generally a conference room of sorts, with a large table and a TV to watch a recording of the show and to be debriefed. Prior to rolling the video, each officer on the team writes down on their debrief sheet all they can recall. Not just from the show they just performed but everything that has transpired since their last team debrief twenty-four hours prior.

The debrief is kicked off with the commanding officer going first, and then it goes down the line, one at a time, through the pilots (both for the jets and our C-130), the maintenance officers, the flight surgeon, supply officer, public affairs officer, on and on from the most senior down to the most junior. Each team member lists everything they did wrong for the entire day and highlight any events where they didn't live up to the responsibility of being a Blue Angel. It could be something as simple as forgetting to take off their sunglasses when they were approached in the parking lot by a young man asking for a picture or an autograph. We believe strongly that eye contact allows for a more personal and intimate connection, so a simple mistake like that is worth highlighting in front of the entire team. The list might also include a safety of flight item from the demonstration, perhaps going lower than was briefed for a particular maneuver. It might take two to three minutes per person, but only after each Blue Angel officer has debriefed their summary for the day do they play the tape and debrief the actual air show.

This debrief is truly one of a kind. It's exceptionally liberating in that each person takes it upon themselves to admit their mistakes and shortcomings to every one of their teammates. This practice allows for a very transparent and effective debrief. The expression "be your own harshest critic" never rings truer than it does in a Blue Angels debrief. When you're able to identify your own failings, it allows for much more effective and faster corrections, and it allows your teammates to in turn do the same. That said, it's not easy. Each person was individually successful before joining the team, and they each have a lot of personal pride in doing well and not making mistakes, so the idea of freely admitting not one but *all* of their mistakes can be daunting initially.

Thankfully, the Blue Angels culture not only allows for it but also encourages it. The magic behind that level of personal accountability is that it truly takes everyone to make it work. It starts with the most senior individual, the commanding officer, and our flight leader, the pilot of the #1 jet. When Boss is able to freely admit his or her mistakes, it eases the burden on the more junior pilots and support officers to do the same.

I mention this because, not surprisingly, this is neither unique nor limited limited to the Blue Angels. The ability to be your own harshest critic is one of the most valuable skills and traits a person can have. I would submit that if you look at people you believe to be highly successful, one trait that many, if not all, have in common is the ability to be introspective, assess successes and failures, and focus their efforts on correcting their failures. We call it situational awareness; some have it, some need it. Situational awareness of self allows for this sort of self-assessment and subsequent improvement.

One of my favorite quotes that seems to capture this in a succinct way is from Norman Vincent Peale, who said, "The trouble with most of us is that we would rather be ruined by praise than saved by criticism." What's also beneficial regardless of your level or ability to assess your weaknesses is having teammates, coworkers, or friends who are willing to help you do so. It's fairly easy to tell someone they've done something right. It takes courage to tell someone they've done something wrong. It's contrary to our human nature, for most of us at least, to look someone in the eye and tell them they erred. It's even harder to make recommendations on how to fix it in the future. That skill set is in short supply, although it's very possible to achieve with dedicated effort.

I would submit that one of the greatest challenges in achieving proper communication in this regard is giving constructive criticism to someone who isn't receptive to it. It's not as simple as just saying the words; they must be formed and delivered in such a way that they don't come off as accusatory or personal but rather intended in a deliberate effort to aid in improvement. For me and I'm sure for many others this wasn't and isn't a simple thing to do. It takes stepping aside and rehearsing the right thing to say and how to properly say it. It might take writing it down or repeating it to yourself silently or aloud in advance. I have found that the more I do this, the easier it gets in the future and the more confident I become in doing so. It takes understanding that delivering constructive criticism is in fact a service to the individual receiving it. It's much easier to not say it at all, to move past and avoid any possible awkwardness, but that doesn't allow for corrections or improvements. Like almost everything, the hard path is the right path; the easy route is that way for a reason, and the result isn't exceptional.

Communication goes both ways. Just as it's a skill to deliver constructive criticism, it's equally challenging to receive it. It starts with being willing to admit your own failures, to be your own harshest critic. That's a start, but not the end. Being able to effectively accept and process constructive criticism from others takes a similar level of confidence and courage. It requires understanding that it's not easy for that person to deliver the critique to you in the first place and that they have also practiced and rehearsed this in a genuine effort to help you improve. If you're able to be empathetic and place yourself in their shoes as you receive this feedback, you'll be more able to accept it. Once again it's the harder path, which means it takes effort, but that effort is worth the reward, the positive change. It's unfair to them if you're unwilling to take that feedback aboard and see it for what it is: a sincere and honest attempt at your individual improvement and the ensuing team's improvement.

Even with the Blue Angels having this culture and dynamic in place, it's always hard and uncomfortable for the newly selected officers to become accustomed to it. It takes days, weeks, sometimes even months for them to be willing to open up and admit all their mistakes. It's clear that the process has worked as intended when someone admits a failure no one else knew about and never would have known about. In that case, it's the clearest and highest form of trust in your teammates and desire to focus on improvement. We watch this transformation happen to each and every Blue Angel officer over the course of their time on our team, and it's magical every time.

Despite it being hard with this culture already in place, it's far more challenging to create this culture somewhere that it doesn't already exist. The simplest and most basic building block is the most senior individual being willing to be vulnerable and confident enough to admit where they failed and how they intend to improve. When the boss, manager, or supervisor is willing to do that in the presence of their employees or subordinates, it almost immediately inculcates that same effective communication culture of the Blue Angels into their team. So if you're trying to take your team to the next level, to make them a higher functioning team, it starts with communicating as a group and being self-aware and confident enough to point the finger at yourself first before turning it on those around you.

For us, communication starts in the jets. It starts with being clear and concise. It requires rehearsal and practice to ensure it's effective. It carries on at the crowd line. It requires believing in your mission, in having the proper message to deliver. It finishes up at the debrief table. It requires the confidence to admit your mistakes and failures. It requires courage to accept constructive criticism with a smile and a genuine willingness to do better, and it requires even more courage to deliver that same constructive criticism to a teammate and a trusted friend or coworker. None of this is impossible to accomplish, and it is highly effective.

CHAPTER 5

ADVERSITY

"It is your reaction to adversity, not the adversity itself, that determines how your life story will develop."

—DIETER UCHTDORF

"PULL YOUR GREEN RING! Pull your green ring!" That came through loud and clear over the radio despite all the other talking between the various jets and the controllers. It was my division leader, one of our squadron's most senior pilots, on a night flight during my first period flying off the aircraft carrier. I had unknowingly fallen victim to hypoxia and was minutes, if not seconds, away from dying as I very much intended to softly land in a nearby swamp so I could get some much-needed rest. Moments later, having pulled the green ring, which resulted in pure oxygen being delivered, I looked outside and said, "Holy shit, I'm flying. And it's nighttime."

How do you deal with adversity in your daily life? How do organizations and teams deal with it? What happens the moment something goes wrong? The world could take a lesson from naval aviation. Let me explain.

When I was traveling the country flying air shows with the Blue Angels, we had the opportunity and the privilege each weekend to visit with groups at the air show location. Typically they were schools and colleges in the local area, but the groups varied and extended as far as civic organizations, hospitals, and various other scheduled events. We weren't there to sign them up to join the military but rather to share our experiences and why we'd each felt called to serve.

To introduce aviation and make some logical connections, I would talk about landing an airplane. I would describe an ideal day—perfect weather, light winds, not a cloud in the sky—and then casually refer to it as a typical day in the life of an Air Force pilot. This served two purposes: one, it usually elicited a laugh and relaxed the group, and two, it reminded (or even instructed) them that the Blue Angels were Navy pilots and not flying in the USAF.

After I showed a picture-perfect day with a nice long runway straight ahead, I would switch to the same picture at night. I would explain how flying is like driving in the sense that nighttime is no different than daytime for the vehicle, be it a car or a plane. But what is very different is the operator's ability to process external information. Nighttime, regardless of your night vision level at any moment, is more challenging because you have significantly reduced visual cues. It's far more challenging to gauge speed changes, closure, direction, and so on. It's significantly harder to merge onto a busy highway at night than it is during the day. It's also significantly harder to land a plane at night for all the same reasons. The picture I showed of a nighttime landing was that nice long runway, right in the city, with buildings lit up all around, a bright runway with glideslope lights, and more all leading the pilot to a safe landing.

I then explained that there's something even harder than landing at nighttime, and it's doing so during the daytime on a moving ship at sea, and I switch to a video. The video is the last 15–20 seconds of an F/A-18 landing on an aircraft carrier. While the video played, I would explain that the Hornet approaches the ship at 141 knots, roughly 165 mph. It's also descending at 720 feet per minute (fpm), and it maintains that descent rate all the way through touchdown, which equates to a *very* noticeable landing. If everything operates as it should and the Hornet catches a wire, one of three or four arresting gear cables, the jet decelerates from 141 knots to a complete stop over the course of 345 feet in under 2 seconds. So it's a bit of a double whammy in the sense that the aircraft is literally crashing into the flight deck at a rate of descent that would open every single overhead compartment on your average commercial plane, in addition to probably dropping all the oxygen masks, and then decelerating at a rate that exceeds even the fastest car braking you've experienced. For those curious, hard braking in a car is defined as decelerating 8–10 mph in 1 second. So, quick math shows that an arresting gear landing from 165 mph to 0 mph in 2 seconds is about ten times more violent than hard braking. The closest most will get to experiencing this is on a roller coaster; but then again, they're along for the ride rather than controlling the ride.

After that video finished, I would show what most believe is a blank, or rather a black, slide. I would say that what they just witnessed is truly an incredible feat in aviation but that, in my opinion, the most challenging aspect in all of aviation is doing that exact thing at night. The screen they were looking at was in fact not a blank screen but rather what a pilot sees when approaching an aircraft carrier at night, and that specific photo was taken from 3 nm behind the boat during a nighttime approach. Because the carrier is usually 100 nm or more from any land, there's no ambient lighting; it's all black. The closest thing I've ever seen to that kind of true darkness is when I was spelunking in my youth while with the Boy Scouts. We were far down in a cave when the guide said, "Okay, shut off your flashlights." For anyone who has experienced that level of darkness, it's truly incredible. That's what the boat offers to those willing to be Navy pilots; it offers total and complete darkness on approach.

At the same approach speed of 141 knots, that 3-mile distance is covered in 1 minute and 16 seconds, and during that time the jet descends from 1,200 feet high to the height of the aircraft carrier flight deck, which is roughly 60 feet above the waterline. The next video I played shows the last 15–20 seconds again, but this time at night, and it was wonderful to watch the reactions of those seeing it for the first time. The aircraft carrier flight deck is kept extremely dark partially out of necessity because a U.S. combat vessel doesn't want to be easily located but also for the benefit of the hundreds of men and women who work on the flight deck all night long. They work in one of if not the most dangerous environments in the world in which there is almost total darkness, and they're surrounded by low-mounted jet engines, turning propellers, and helicopter rotor blades in every direction. Maintaining night vision is critical for their safety, so as much as we might want a well-lit runway to land on, their safety is paramount.

As the video began to take its effect, I would mention that what they just watched is a night carrier landing in good weather. It's the bad weather days, the days with a pitching deck due to high seas, that really get your blood pumping as a Navy pilot. Unfortunately, any video from those days wouldn't be much to watch because you'd literally see nothing at all. In those instances, it's the men and women working as landing signals officers who earn their pay through exceptional performance, as made clear when we were discussing trust.

And so let us go back to adversity and how to deal with it. The truth is, no matter how challenging it might be to land a plane at night on a moving ship at sea, there's something still more challenging. And that is doing that exact same thing with an airplane that isn't working properly, which, of course, could be any number of things. For example, if the radios stop working, we have procedures for what to do; but there's always this great unknown in terms of trusting that the procedures will work and ensuring that everyone knows what's happening and that the airplane that isn't talking to anyone is in fact NORDO (no operating radio). Losing your avionics or your electrical system is even more troubling because the flight information provided is critical to safe flight. Finally, any sort of hydraulic or engine failure can so drastically reduce the aircraft's performance that landing it can prove very challenging—the tolerance for mistakes is almost nonexistent because most airplanes don't have the power or flight control stability to recover once the pilot has made too large of an error in power or flight control input.

So what happens when things go wrong? As I mentioned to begin with, naval aviation and even aviation in general has an incredible way of dealing with adversity built off a hundred years of lessons learned in an arena that is unforgiving and never the same.

Prior to ever getting airborne in a new aircraft, each pilot spends weeks studying the systems, almost to the point that they could have been the engineer who designed them. This is often the source of much consternation, and comments like "You pay me to fly this thing, not build it" are routinely heard during ground school. Once each pilot has studied and been tested on everything from the engines to the hydraulic system, the flight control system, the electrical systems, and so on, it's time to study what could go wrong. These are commonly referred to as emergency procedures, or EPs. Depending on the complexity of the aircraft, or even the size and mission of the aircraft, the list might be long or it might be quite short and straightforward. EPs are also studied and assessed on both the likelihood of happening and the severity of the impact they each have.

For example, when I joined, new pilots were flying the T-34C Turbo Mentor (now replaced by the T-6A Texan II). The T-34C was a single-engine turboprop in which the two aircrew sit in tandem, meaning one directly behind the other with the instructor pilot typically in the back seat. As you might expect, the most critical emergency you might experience in a single-engine airplane is the loss of that engine. Any number of things might make the engine quit: mechanical failures, structural failures, fuel starvation or contamination, loss of oil, bird strike, and more, but that's somewhat irrelevant the moment it quits.

What is relevant is knowing the procedures when it does. This particular EP gets so much attention that after having flown that plane for only six months over twenty years ago, I can still recite what to do as if I were flying it yesterday. The second the engine quits, we would say to ourselves, "100, clean, check, feather, look, lock, airstart, bailout." Those are all immediate items, but they must be addressed one at a time. That said, any delays might prohibit you from getting the airplane down safely. What those memory items actually mean are as follows:

1. Flying speed—MAINTAIN (100 KIAS [knots indicated airspeed] minimum)
2. Landing gear and flaps—UP
3. Engine instruments—CHECK
4. Condition lever—FEATHER (as required)
5. Landing site—SELECT
6. Harness—LOCKED
7. Airstart—PERFORM (if situation permits)
8. No landing site available and altitude permits—BAILOUT

Critical in the execution is that each of the first steps happen in order or the rest of the steps are irrelevant. For example, if you don't fly and trim the aircraft to the precise speed, then none of the other steps matter because you'll get so slow without the power the engine normally produces that you will put the aircraft in a position where it stalls or spins, and then you've compounded the emergency to a point that the rest of the items don't matter. What I mean is that it's not necessary to check your instruments if you're in a spin and rapidly descending to the ground; at that point your new EP is Unintentional Spin (power idle, controls release, rudder full against spin, etc.). Next in order is the landing gear position. If you don't ensure the gear and flaps are up, you'll never achieve the expected glide ratio to your intended landing spot because the drag from either of those two items will vastly increase your rate of descent. The list goes on, and if you get so far as to decide you have a suitable landing spot, there's a bit more you're required to remember:

1. Emergency Engine Shutdown—EXECUTE
2. MAYDAY/7700—BROADCAST
3. ELP (emergency landing pattern)—INTERCEPT
4. Gear and flaps—AS REQUIRED
5. Canopy—EMERGENCY OPEN
6. Battery switch—OFF

And that's just one of the sixty-four EPs for the T-34C. The point is, there is a lot of studying, a lot of memorization, and a lot of preparation before you ever sit in the cockpit of an aircraft. Moreover, after you study and are tested on all the systems and the EPs, each pilot spends weeks in the simulator to ensure they know where all those aforementioned switches are and to get really familiar with the aircraft before finding themselves airborne, dealing with an emergency, and feeling unsure how exactly to do some of the otherwise simple items.

I give you that background so you can consider how this might relate to your own life. How does it relate to your job, your hobbies, even your day-to-day activities? I would submit that most of us simply go through the motions. We go about our day with little, if any, forethought as to what could go wrong. Naturally, when something does go wrong, we address it in the moment and hopefully move on, no worse for the wear. But sometimes, of course, we are worse off, and we find ourselves at a new low or disadvantage because of what happened and how we dealt with it.

Imagine if you took the time to make a list of what might go wrong in your daily life or at work. Imagine if you took it one step further and listed out the most effective steps in dealing with that event. Finally, imagine if you took the time to refine that list every time something went wrong in an attempt to arrive at the best and most effective solution to that problem. How many people do you know or work with who put in that amount of time and deliberate action to dealing with adversity? I would guess that it's very few, if any.

I would also acknowledge that certainly most of us in our daily activities aren't in immediate life-or-death situations when things go wrong. Not every aircraft emergency is a life-or-death situation, but that still doesn't mean we don't give those emergencies the same level of focus or attention as those that are more time critical or potentially devastating.

As I stated in the beginning, some of these concepts to deal with adversity aren't revolutionary, but actually doing what is required to mitigate negative consequences is to some degree revolutionary because so few people take the time to do it. What's very likely is that when you see people around you succeeding and accelerating in their careers or their hobbies, it's not by magic but perhaps because they make fewer mistakes. Moreover, when they do have things go wrong, they capitalize on them through direct attention rather than being hobbled by them. Being ready and prepared for adversity, then acting on it appropriately might not even be recognizable, but for those willing to approach adversity properly, the result is success in their chosen endeavor.

Back to the story I started the chapter with. When I finished flight school, I was kept at the same squadron where I received my wings to be a flight instructor, or SERGRAD (selectively retained graduate), for the next eighteen months before moving to NAS Oceana in Virginia Beach, Virginia, where I learned how to fly the F/A-18. As a flight instructor, I flew constantly, normally three times a day, six days a week. I went from having 300 hours to 1,500 hours in just over a year, and my experiences during that time positively affected my next twenty years of flying. When I showed up to my first squadron at NAS Oceana, I was the most junior member of our ready room and our group of fifteen F/A-18 pilots, and I was a "nugget," which is naval aviation's term for those who haven't completed a carrier deployment. I joined the squadron, VFA-87, as it was finishing workups, which is the predeployment training cycle.

Almost immediately after joining the squadron we were out at sea for a month, off the coast of NAS Jacksonville, training and preparing for the combat deployment that would start a few months later. We flew daily in various exercises and missions to ensure the aircrew, the carrier, and the supporting strike group were ready for any number of different and unexpected scenarios. One such mission was a nighttime strike of an inland land target. Despite these being training missions into approved U.S. bombing ranges, we treated them with as much realism as we possibly could. For example, on this training sortie we had four F/A-18s flying as our Blue Air, or good guys, and multiple other airplanes simulating the Red Air, or bad guys. Simulating our enemies can be challenging; in doing so it's critical to present an accurate and realistic presentation of what we could expect. Sometimes the Red Air presentation was very challenging if that mission was meant to engage with an experienced and credible threat, and other times the presentation was less challenging in simulating a far less experienced airborne threat.

In this instance our four airplanes planned and briefed our mission, which was to drop inert (nonexplosive) ordnance into Pinecastle, a bombing range south of Jacksonville, Florida, and west of Daytona Beach. We briefed to a possible airborne threat, that is enemy aircraft with which we might engage, and how we would address each possible situation whether we encountered them en route to our target or on our way back or, worst case, at both times. The U.S. military does an exceptional job of training; the mantra "we sweat in training, so we don't bleed in combat" is stated quite often. In preparing to deploy to the Persian Gulf a few months later and flying combat missions over Iraq, we didn't anticipate any airborne threats, but that didn't mean we didn't train for them. Quite the opposite—we trained to encounter the most challenging and experienced threats imaginable because if we didn't, we wouldn't properly be prepared.

This obviously goes back to the discussion of EPs, and it's the training and tactical equivalent of being prepared for things to go wrong or for the unexpected to happen. If you're properly prepared for it, dealing with and addressing an issue isn't an emergency but rather just standard operations. If we as a country want to prevent ourselves from ever being invaded, much less defeated, we must constantly prepare, train, and equip ourselves to encounter and defeat the most challenging and imposing threats.

So when the time came, we put on our gear and headed to the flight deck, flashlights in hand. What should be a simple act of preflighting an F/A-18 is substantially more challenging on the flight deck of an aircraft carrier at night. Each pilot knows what aspects of his plane to check prior to climbing in. We always make sure the intake areas for each engine are clear of any objects that might get sucked in and damage the motor, we verify that each of the many doors are closed properly and secured, we check the tires and the brakes for wear and tear, and so on. Doing this on a flight deck with other aircraft taxing and turning is far more dangerous. E-2 Hawkeyes have turning propellers, helicopters are all around you with turning rotor blades, and depending on your timing, you might be in the middle of a launch or landing cycle, which increases the risks even more.

After a complete preflight inspection, I climbed the ladder and strapped into my F/A-18C for the night training mission. As a brand-new pilot to the squadron, I hadn't flown the instructional flights required to fly with night vision goggles (NVGs). Normally, once you were airborne and climbing away from the aircraft carrier and the water, each pilot would attach his NVGs, and the darkness would go away immediately. Although everything displayed is a shade of green, and despite them functioning proportionally with how much light is available from the moon and the stars, they are a huge improvement from the alternative where everything is just black. They allow you to see aircraft from long distances away and fly safe formation as well.

Because I hadn't had the training yet, we briefed to the fact that I would be the only one of the four in our division who wasn't using NVGs, and as such everyone would be a bit wary of the new guy who wasn't just inexperienced but also couldn't see anything. Not a great position to be in. Furthermore, I was in the fourth position, which is usually the position of the most junior member of the formation. The leader of our division was a very experienced pilot and a lieutenant commander and department head in our squadron, and he was responsible for me and the other two wingmen.

Off we went, proceeding inbound to drop our inert ordnance on our target at the exact prebriefed time. There were a variety of simulated enemy aircraft between us and the target, but as a division of fighters, we prosecuted the threats using our jets' ability to simulate missile launches and to track the simulated missiles through their time of flight. Having successfully eliminated the enemy air threat, we proceeded into the target area, and we each, in order, dropped our bombs. As we came off target and climbed away to rejoin as a formation, I was overwhelmed by a sense of fatigue and confusion. I heard the comm that is used to redress our formation by our lead aircraft, and I heard the controller advising us of additional enemy aircraft that were inbound. Despite hearing that, all I could think about at that moment was that I was tired and needed a short rest.

That feeling should have been the last thing I was thinking about at that moment because just being in a fighter is exhilarating, and having launched off an aircraft carrier at night, shooting down enemy aircraft, and dropping ordnance onto a target are the sorts of things that require a high degree of concentration and focus. It typically takes hours to calm down to the point of being able to sleep after that sort of event.

Despite that, I was so exhausted in that moment that I said on the radio, "Hey, I'm tired. I'm just going to go back and rest." My section leader, the third member of our formation, was about as confused as anyone could possibly be, and he said something to the effect of "What? What are you talking about?" In the moment all I could think about was going back to Pinecastle, that big target that was just a large swampy area in north-central Florida, and softly landing my airplane in the swamp and getting some much-needed rest. I replied, "Yep, I'm just gonna go get some rest." You can probably imagine both his confusion and surprise, especially coupled with the fact that I was the new guy and not on NVGs. There was a moment of confusion while the division lead was reorienting our formation and preparing us for the enemy aircraft, and the controllers were announcing their position and heading and altitude. I was oblivious now to most everything and slowly turned away, not really sure where I was going.

In that moment, our division lead unquestionably saved my life. He keyed his mic and said, "Pull your green ring. Pull your green ring. Pull your green ring," over and over again. The green ring in our jets was a small ring to the left of our left thigh, and it was our emergency oxygen actuator. Pulling it allows for ten minutes of pure oxygen to get routed to the mask and cuts off the supply of air we normally receive from our On-Board Oxygen Generating System (OBOGS). OBOGS is an ingenious invention that allows pilots to have air to breath indefinitely in our jets—prior to its integration we carried a ten-liter canister of liquid oxygen (LOX) in the plane. If you had a long flight and used up the LOX, you ran out of breathable air and became very limited in what altitude you could fly, meaning you were relegated to being at low altitudes for the remainder of the flight and weren't able to wear your mask, all of which are very undesirable while flying a jet. The OBOGS had some hiccups along the way, but in general it is a terrific system.

In the moments after I heard Kevin "Major" Healy calling for me to pull my green ring, I vaguely remember wondering who he was talking to and why he kept saying the same thing. Almost as if it were the only way to make him be quiet, and in a close to totally mindless state, I pulled my green ring. In virtually an instant I was completely in control of my faculties and knew exactly where I was and what I was doing. I went from having no clue where I was and seconds away from falling permanently asleep behind the controls of an F/A-18 out at sea to saying, "Holy shit, I'm flying. And it's nighttime." The effect of pure oxygen was an instant fix for what had been a malfunctioning OBOGS that was delivering an incorrect mixture of air, resulting in me being essentially poisoned and subsequently hypoxic.

Hypoxia is an incredibly dangerous part of flying tactical aircraft because the altitudes can change in seconds from a point where you could breathe normally with outside, ambient air at sea level (or even 5,000–10,000 feet) to being at 30,000 or 40,000 feet high. Anyone exposed to that thin air and being deprived of either LOX- or OBOGS-provided air has mere seconds of useful consciousness. Many Hornet pilots and other tactical pilots over the years have perished while flying, in many cases with no known cause or explanation. I would submit that many of those cases were possibly if not even likely caused by some form of hypoxia; and as such, the military in general and aviation at a macro level have responded with training, education, and better systems.

In the Navy we're given annual training that covers the factors that lead to hypoxia and the symptoms to recognize its onset. We're given simulator training while wearing reduced oxygen breathing devices so we can best understand how we perform in that type of environment. Even with all that training and education, it's still incredibly hard to predict how each person will respond in that environment as the effect of hypoxia is different on everyone. One aspect of hypoxia that makes it so dangerous is its insidious onset. Typically, it shows up in the form of decreased night vision or even mild drowsiness. These are somewhat normal experiences when operating late at night or outside of your normal circadian rhythms, so feeling that way is not necessarily unexpected. Following symptoms are confusion, poor judgment, loss of muscle coordination, then eventually total loss of consciousness. Some who are under the effects of hypoxia might have discolored lips or blue nails, which would be easy to self-diagnose if it weren't for the fact that an oxygen mask covers half our face and thus our lips, and we typically fly with gloves that cover the nails.

For me that evening, my symptoms were all too typical: fatigue, some dizziness, and even light nausea. In the moment, I just wanted to get some much-needed rest, and I fully intended to do just that were it not for someone screaming to pull my green ring. I don't recall when during that flight I started to feel bad. I'm sure it was sometime before I announced I was leaving, but once again because of the insidious nature of hypoxia, I wasn't able to diagnose myself early enough to fix it.

As I came to my senses and announced what had happened and explained my physical condition, it was decided that I should return to the carrier for assistance. That evening, due to the severity of what had just happened, our commanding officer, the skipper, left the squadron ready room and proceeded to the Carrier Air Traffic Control Center (CATCC) so he could talk through the ship's radios directly to me. Usually we assign various pilots in the squadron to be on duty to assist with anyone who is airborne and needs help with any variety of anomalies or emergencies. In this case, the skipper coming personally signified the seriousness of the situation. I explained what had happened, and we walked through the EP while I made my way back the 100 nm to the carrier.

We weren't sure yet what exactly caused me to become hypoxic, but we went through the Hornet's procedures that were available to us. The procedure at the time was to remove your mask and stow the green ring once the hypoxic symptoms had subsided. It was a recognized benefit of the newer Hornets, which I was flying, that you could stow the green ring, allowing the remaining air to be available later. The earliest Hornets didn't have that capability, so from the moment you pulled the handle, you had ten minutes, then the emergency oxygen was depleted and that was it. So I removed my mask and discussed with my skipper the plan of returning to the ship: descend to the approach altitude of 1,200 feet and only put my mask back on when I was a few minutes from landing and fly the last few minutes using the emergency oxygen.

With the commanding officer sitting in CATCC and awaiting my arrival, I did as instructed. As I descended to 1,200 feet, still feeling a bit queasy and generally miserable, I prepared for the final approach, and when I found myself 3 nm behind the boat, just a few minutes prior to landing, I reattached my mask, felt the flow of air, and pushed over to begin the final descent to land. That period of 3 nm only takes 1 minute and 17 seconds, but in that short time, I immediately began to lose any understanding of what I was doing. I vaguely remember responding to a few radio calls, seeing the carrier deck lights, and even seeing the IFLOLS (Improved Fresnel Lens Optical Landing System) to the left of the landing area that gives us our glideslope information. Despite that, within about half a mile and only 10–15 seconds prior to landing, I was able to make out two, if not three, separate aircraft carriers all sort of spinning around each other. My thought, though incapacitated at the time, was "that ain't right," and I took my own wave off, meaning without being instructed to I added power and discontinued the approach, flying directly over the ship in a straight ahead climb. Almost immediately someone asked me what was wrong, and I replied, "I feel awful." Our skipper, who had been watching the entire episode, was up on the radio instantly: "Did you pull your green ring?" I looked down to see that in fact, no, the green ring was stowed, just as I'd left it. I pulled it out and again, almost instantaneously, I had 100 percent oxygen forced into my mask and I had my faculties back. I knew where I was, and I knew I needed to turn downwind to get set up for another approach. I just didn't know why I hadn't pulled the green ring when I should have.

After successfully landing the second time around, thankfully without further incident, we were able to remove the OBOGS and debrief the entire ordeal. It became apparent to me once I was no longer flying and able to better evaluate my actions that my most critical mistake was donning my mask, feeling normal airflow, and assuming it was good to go. I had, without knowing it at the time, started over the process of breathing in poisoned air, and since my body hadn't had any time to go through its normal process of recovering, I was almost immediately incapacitated yet again.

One of the things aviation excels at, especially military aviation, is learning from its mistakes and improving its processes for future operations. In this case, we not only had the OBOGS sent away for inspection, but we debriefed at length my actions and what led to not only the first hypoxic incident but the second as well. There was no question that I didn't recognize the symptoms or the onset, really either time, and certainly not well enough to take the correct action. It was also obvious that when I put my mask on prior to landing, having felt normal airflow, I incorrectly assumed it was good air, certainly not poisoned air. As a result of this incident, and I suspect others, our procedures in the Hornet changed significantly over the following years. Notably the procedure now includes turning off the flow knob to the OBOGS once the aircrew has ascertained that the system is malfunctioning so they're no longer able to ingest any more air that's not emergency oxygen.

It was determined the OBOGS had malfunctioned and not produced the right percentages of air, thus leading to the hypoxic symptoms. The Navy's system of reporting allowed us to file a HAZREP, a report of a hazardous situation, which is disseminated to all squadrons with similar systems. We heard back from other Hornet squadrons, both Navy and Marine, that upon subsequent inspections, they found similar malfunctioning units.

These processes allow us to deal with adversity and not let it defeat us. We're constantly working to better educate and train our crews and improve our systems. In this case, it wasn't in any way, shape, or form my ability to deal with adversity that saved my life but rather the ability of a more seasoned pilot who took immediate and quick action to ensure I was okay. It further proves the importance of having a good wingman. We're all susceptible to mistakes, and in aviation mistakes often come at a higher cost, so a little help from our friends sometimes can go a *long* way.

Thankfully having experienced that and survived, I was well positioned to self-diagnose when I felt that way on subsequent flights, which certainly happened over the next fifteen years flying Hornets. On multiple occasions my oxygen system functioned improperly, and mild nausea or fatigue was an immediate red flag for me that would immediately prompt me to level off, remove my mask, and assess what system had malfunctioned to give me those symptoms. Sadly, not everyone was lucky enough to have a senior aviator with them to immediately make the perfect call—clear and concise—that ultimately saved my life.

Hopefully that illustrates the importance and critical nature of knowing what to do in case of an emergency. That's not all that's required for dealing with adversity, however. Knowing what to do is one aspect, but handling it the right way is something different altogether, and its applicability extends far beyond aviation.

Some of the very best advice I ever received in terms of dealing with adversity was to underreact. Not react, certainly not overreact, but to very deliberately underreact and do so in an almost extreme manner. This applies to nearly everything: human interactions, market twists and turns, even airborne emergencies. Let me explain what I mean by underreacting in the extreme.

Picture yourself once again in an airplane; it could be a highly maneuverable F/A-18 or almost its opposite, an extremely stable Airbus 350. As you're flying along you begin getting indications of erratic engine readings, then almost immediately you get indications of an engine fire on your right engine. In either case you have only two engines, so they're both somewhat critical to safely operating your aircraft, although the aircraft can certainly be flown and landed, albeit with a greater degree of difficulty and risk, with only one engine. You know exactly what you're supposed to do because you've gone through the required training, you've memorized exactly which buttons to push and in which order, so what comes next shouldn't be that hard. How, then, is it possible that despite hours, days, even months of study, practice, and simulators that so many pilots in both fighter jets and large commercial and corporate aircraft in very similar situations shut off their good and fully functional engine rather than the one that's on fire?

That answer is as simple and logical as you might expect. They panicked or hurried or otherwise rushed through a procedure that didn't require that level of immediacy. The airplane would have continued to fly safely with the pilot or aircrew doing exactly nothing, in fact. An engine on fire could possibly cause other complications, but often it will just burn itself out, so shutting it down in a hurry rather than a minute later certainly won't save any appreciable amount of money in repair costs. The point is the immediacy of it shouldn't even be a consideration. Yet still, a good many pilots in this situation will react, even possibly overreact, when they should be underreacting.

To understand underreacting in the extreme, picture yourself in a Hornet. Your engine is on fire, and it seems nearly every warning light in the cockpit has instantly lit up. How do we brief what to do next? It's as simple as underreacting. Often we brief something to the effect of "no fast hands in the cockpit," and other times it's "sit on your hands and take a deep breath." In practice this allows you to process the entire situation, not just the first warning light you saw. In many cases, the first thing that goes wrong catches your eye, but it's just an indication or symptom of a much larger issue. If you react to the first light rather than taking a deep breath and understanding fully what is going on, you might miss seeing that the actual problem is something different altogether. It might sound crazy, almost irrational, to consider yourself in a fighter with an engine on fire and taking a breath and sitting on your hands, but that simple act would have saved many planes from being lost over the years.

Now picture yourself in a massive Airbus A350 taking off from San Francisco and heading to Tokyo. Almost immediately after takeoff the same thing happens, right engine fire. How does a well-trained professional crew handle this very similar emergency? The pilot not flying the aircraft calmly states, "Our right engine is on fire," while the pilot flying the aircraft continues flying and instructs him or her to go through the engine fire checklist. They follow all the same procedures and as they proceed through the checklist, at some point it will call to secure, or shut off, the engine that is on fire or otherwise not functioning. Prior to either member of the crew moving a switch that shuts off fuel, one person will state, "I show that the left engine is operating normally, and I'm covering up the fuel switch for the operating engine." The comm varies slightly by aircraft type and model, but the idea is the same. There is no rush and no immediacy, and they will go to great lengths to not inadvertently shut off the known good engine as that would certainly result in a very unfortunate situation.

That is the aviation example of underreacting in the extreme. When a situation arises that could easily cause the loss of an aircraft and perhaps the loss of one or hundreds of individuals, rather than panicking or overreacting, the crew remains calm and collected and executes slowly and with total control. That same thing can be done in almost any situation, and it's almost always the proper response. Looking back, how many times have you reacted quickly or overreacted and thought, "Wow, I'm glad I overreacted to that situation; that certainly helped fix that problem"? I would submit it's probably none.

Another perfect example of underreacting in the extreme occurred in a squadron that had experienced a mishap, the loss of an aircraft. This is a commanding officer's absolute worst nightmare and is almost always an immediate career-ending situation. In this case, the commanding officer was immediately made aware of a mishap, the jet was lost, the pilot alive, and a trusted mentor told him to come with him. They went on a short drive around the base, not terribly long but just long enough to allow the commanding officer, the skipper of the squadron, to remove himself from the situation, the emotion, the lack of details, and instead focus on the bigger picture. Just a few minutes of focus and clarity replaced what would have certainly been him micromanaging a response through a well-intentioned but misplaced need for immediate answers though none were available. It allowed focus and perspective to replace an overreaction to adversity. It was certainly the leadership equivalent of "no fast hands in the cockpit," and as it turned out, it worked. It allowed him to have clarity, control, and the ability to lead his squadron, his command, through a terrible and tragic ordeal. It only took a moment, but it took an extreme underreaction.

All these stories and anecdotes remind me of one of my favorite quotes by Andy Grove, the CEO of Intel. He said, "Bad companies are destroyed by crisis. Good companies survive them. Great companies are improved by them." This encapsulates my personal experience and these examples better than any quote I've ever heard. If you're able to properly and professionally prepare for adversity, there are no crises, and moreover, if you're able to learn from your mistakes, they absolutely only make you stronger and more effective. The trick is that it takes deliberate action; it takes effort and foresight rather than simply going through the motions and reacting to what hand life deals you. If you're able to properly communicate and make yourself vulnerable while you share your failings, that is your personal failings and those of your team, then you are set up to succeed. If you have the situational awareness to recognize where you fall short, and if you're willing to take the constructive criticism of those around you, then you're well positioned to improve and improve dramatically. So many are unable and unwilling to put themselves in that position, so those who are willing have very little standing between them and unimaginable success.

The Blue Angels Solo pilots have a trademark maneuver known as the High Alpha Pass. It's a maneuver where both aircraft slow down to a speed that's so incredibly low, the jets stand on their tails while flying in front of the crowd. Their flight attitude appears as if they're in a very steep climb, but they are in fact flying at a precise altitude, not climbing or descending, straight down the show line. Normally the jets are going between 400 and 500 mph as they pass by the crowd, but in this case, they are going barely over 100 mph, giving the spectators plenty of time to take photographs and wonder how a fighter jet can fly so low.

As it turns out, flying slow is quite a tactical advantage for a jet whose purpose is maintaining an aerial advantage. The SEALs have an expression they've become known for, which is to "never bring a knife to a gunfight." They have a lot of credibility in this department, and the meaning is not twofold; it's probably tenfold or a millionfold for them. The first time I heard that quote, however, was from Sean Connery (as Jim Malone) to Kevin Costner (as Elliott Ness) in *The Untouchables.* As it relates to fighters, it's generally expected that any jet worth its salt is extremely fast, and that's partially true. That said, if two jets end up within visual range of each other, it's no longer a fight with long-range missiles guided by radars but rather a very personal and intimate fighter pilot battle. We use the expression that a dogfight at that close range becomes more of a knife fight in a phone booth.

In that situation, the ability for your jet to fly slowly is of the utmost importance. When you're that close to another jet, the ability to go exceptionally fast is only helpful if you intend to run away and hopefully outrun a missile that is headed up your tailpipe. If you want to defeat the enemy, then you must maneuver to his six—that is, end up behind him—so you can use your forward-firing ordnance, possibly even your gun to shoot him down. The Hornet does that better than most any aircraft, which makes it a very respectable adversary in the visual arena. On the Blue Angels we look to showcase what our jet does best, and because that's one of its absolute greatest strengths, we demonstrate and display that for the crowd.

Not only do we stand a jet on its tail, but we do it in very close formation. That demonstrates not only what the jet can do but that it can do it with a high degree of control and precision, which is the ultimate compliment to that jet. Flying an aircraft to the edge of its envelope is challenging; doing it close to the ground is even more challenging because of the increased risk. Doing it close to the ground and inches away from another aircraft is an absolute exclamation point in what it is capable of doing, and that maneuver, the Section High Alpha Pass, is flown at each and every Blue Angels air show.

The degree of risk versus reward is present each demonstration. In 2010 a Canadian F/A-18 was performing the same maneuver, but as a single aircraft rather than in formation, at the Alberta International Air Show in Alberta, Canada. In the middle of the maneuver, with the jet almost directly in front of the crowd, the right engine failed, resulting in an immediate loss of altitude and an uncontrolled roll-off to the right. The pilot ejected with milliseconds to spare and parachuted down narrowly missing the inferno that was the burning F/A-18 below him. This mishap, more than almost any other, demonstrates the risks associated with air shows because this particular failure is easily recoverable if it happens at 10,000 feet in a simulated dogfight with another aircraft. However, at 200 feet it's almost totally unrecoverable and a half second of delay can lead to the catastrophic loss of an aircraft.

That year, 2010, I was the Lead Solo on the Blue Angels and flew that same maneuver each and every day, except I did it in formation a mere few feet away from another jet. As fate would have it, we experienced a similar mishap that year at an air show over Lake Michigan flown over the great city of Milwaukee. In our case, we were at the very end of the maneuver, having flown slowly in front of the crowd all the way down the show line. For our typical end to that maneuver the Lead Solo would transmit "wave it off," which would direct the wingman, the Opposing Solo, to advance his throttles to full afterburner and maintain the same backstick pull, which with the massive thrust increase would cause the aircraft to climb in an almost purely vertical display. Meanwhile the Lead Solo would also select full afterburner but instead accelerate straight ahead demonstrating the incredible climb versus acceleration profiles of the two jets. On this day in Michigan, as I selected full afterburner, my engine didn't fail as was the case at the Canadian air show; I flew through a flock of birds.

Generally speaking, birds don't pose much of a risk to fighters. Our typical missions and training sorties occur at altitudes at which birds can't fly, so they're typically only a concern in takeoff and landing environments. Unfortunately, air show flight profiles are in the heart of the envelope for the flight paths of most birds, so they become a legitimate hazard. Many airports and air shows go to great lengths to deter birds using a variety of methods to keep them away, both for their safety and the safety of the airplanes.

The minute I hit the first bird, I knew it was bad. My jet was in a compromised state already. I was low and slow, exactly where you never want to be. Not only that—I was low and slow and now experiencing an engine failure. It's funny what you think of during times like this. Many people who have been in car crashes explain their experience of time compression; the idea that a car accident that lasted a few seconds or even fractions of a second felt like minutes or hours. Time slowed down in their mind, and they processed things at such a high rate it felt like it lasted forever.

For me in this case, I had two immediate thoughts. The first, for some insanely stupid reason, was I recalled a scene from *Indiana Jones and the Last Crusade* where Indiana (Harrison Ford) and his father, Henry Jones Sr. (Sean

Connery) were being attacked by an airplane, and in an attempt to save them Henry Sr. stirred up a beach full of birds. The birds flew into the sky and caused the airplane to crash because, as he stated, "I suddenly remembered my Charlemagne. Let my armies be the rocks and the trees and the birds in the sky." Remembering that movie in that moment wasn't the slightest bit helpful, but I did feel like I shared some bizarre experience with the fictitious pilot in that movie of flying through a flock of birds. My next thought was equally unhelpful, which was, "Crap, I don't feel like getting wet today." Our air show was flown directly over the lake, and as I flew through that flock of birds and watched every warning light in my jet go off almost instantly, I couldn't help but think of how cold Lake Michigan probably was and how my Georgia upbringing in no way prepared me for ending up in that lake, freezing to death, even if I was lucky enough to survive the ejection.

Thankfully for me, I had receive years of exceptional training and muscle memory kicked in. I had already "dumped the nose," or pushed forward on the stick to accelerate, because that was that portion of our maneuver and my engines were already being advanced to full power, so my only responsibility at that point was to stomp on the rudder pedal to counteract the yawing motion that comes from losing your engine and to maintain a steady, albeit very slight, climb to ensure I safely got away from the water. Luck was further on my side being over a lake as there weren't any trees or other obstructions that are so prevalent at other shows, so my slight climb attitude was still safe and manageable. Finally, the last portion of this maneuver was proper communication. For the first and only time in over ten years of flying with the Blue Angels, I called a "Knock it off," which was our comm term for everything stops. All Blue Angel maneuvering ceases to allow the aircraft in distress to have absolute free range to maneuver as required. That meant the diamond that was already turning in for their next maneuver immediately turned away in the opposite direction, allowing me the ability to maneuver as required to safely establish my flight path toward our landing field. In yet another case of good luck, despite being over the lake rather than an airfield, our air show airport was Milwaukee Mitchell airport, the main Milwaukee airport, and it was 5 nm away from our show center, which gave me just enough time to turn, establish myself on final, and land as the rest of the aircraft systems failed due to the compounded emergencies that resulted from the flock of birds and the destruction they enacted on my jet.

This day proved to me so many aspects about dealing with adversity. First and foremost, it reaffirmed for me the importance of knowing your procedures and executing them as trained. It also showed me that not immediately ejecting but rather taking a moment to process the situation and letting the aircraft decide if it had the ability and power to climb away produced a favorable result. Most importantly, all the other people involved—my wingman (the Opposing Solo) assisting me, our Boss (the flight leader) quickly maneuvering his formation away from my position, our Comm Cart rapidly liaising with a major international airport to make them aware of my unexpected and emergency return—did exactly what they were taught to do. They did it with focus, with clear and concise communication, and with the professionalism of Blue Angels, which allowed for the safe recovery of an aircraft that could have easily been lost to the lake that day. It takes a team, not an individual, to execute like that, and in that moment I was proud to call myself a Blue Angel and proud to be surrounded by so many exceptional individuals.

Allow me to share one final vignette. I had the opportunity in my first year on the Blue Angels to give hundreds of backseat rides. That year I was the team's narrator, so during the air shows I would stand in front of the crowd and narrate our entire hour-long ground and airborne demonstration. As a pilot, my job was to give backseat rides to a variety of individuals. Some were celebrities; others were influential in the lives of young adults. They varied day by day.

One of my backseat riders was a gentleman named Brian Terwilliger. A few years before we met, he made a movie titled *One Six Right: The Romance of Flying* about aviation in general but specifically about Runway 16R at Van Nuys in Southern California. His movie had developed almost a cult following among aviation afficionados, and the Blue Angels offered him a backseat ride. He subsequently made a short film called *Flying Full Circle* about his experience with us. Years later Brian went on to write, direct, and produce an IMAX documentary titled *Living in the Age of Airplanes* that was an immediate success.

Brian and I kept up over the years and reconnected at the Sun 'n Fun air show shortly after the IMAX film came out. As we caught up, he shared some stories of the film and what went in to getting it on the big, the really big, IMAX screen. He needed funding and as such went to some of the biggest names in all of aviation. During one pitch meeting, as he went through his presentation, his clicker slipped out of his hand and hit the floor. The noise it made was loud enough that basically everyone in the room heard it and knew what had happened. Brian continued with his presentation, reached into his jacket pocket, and pulled out his spare remote. After he'd wrapped up, the gentleman he was presenting to stopped him and said, "Sorry to stop you for a second, but did you just pull a spare remote out of your jacket?" Brian acknowledged what had happened, and later explained to me that the gentleman was ultimately as surprised and impressed with the level of preparedness as he was with the actual presentation. Brian's ability to anticipate what might go wrong and prepare for it in advance demonstrated not just his ability to deal with adversity in a deal pitch but was illustrative of how he lived his life. That single, somewhat simple action was more than enough to prove that every detail, both big and small, would be addressed and that everything that could go wrong would have a plan, a backup plan, and would be executed in such a seamless and transparent way as to hide it from all but the most astute observers.

When Brian and I flew together, we were both interviewed for what would become the short film *Flying Full Circle*, and it was in that film that Brian discussed what led him to being invited to fly with the Blue Angels. His response was absolutely perfect as he said how fortunate he felt to fly with the team and remarked, "The luck is really preparation meeting opportunity."

That sentiment perfectly summarizes my thoughts on dealing with adversity. Life throws us curveballs each and every day. Some are mere annoyances, and others can be crushing. What defines us isn't the curveball we're thrown but how we respond to it, how we play the hand we're dealt. Brian's preparation was no different than him being ready with the second clicker; it was no different than thousands of pilots studying and rehearsing their EPs over and over. They all hoped they'd never have to find themselves in a position to have to recall them but knew they wanted to be ready should it be required. If you're properly prepared, then there are no emergencies, just a few of life's curveballs that you can knock out of the park.

CHAPTER 6

FAILURE

"We are all failures—at least the best of us are."

—J. M. BARRIE

"Wave off! Wave off!" our landing signals officer, the LSO screamed at me through the radio. That call is never said in a conversational manner. As I discussed in the communication chapter, we can communicate with our words and our delivery; and in this case, the situation is extreme and dire enough that these words are almost always shouted to magnify the seriousness of the situation.

Despite my failure that resulted in being screamed at, I did at least do the next part right. We're taught when learning how to land on the aircraft carrier that if we hear "wave off," we should add full power, not land, and instead go around for another approach. Unfortunately for me in this case, I did land, and I enjoyed what felt like a forever taxi into the carrier's #1 wire. What that all means is that I was, in a metaphorical sense, far enough behind the jet that although I was in the cockpit physically, I was barely hanging onto the tail mentally. Had I not been told to wave off and immediately added power, I would have very likely ended up crashing into the back of the boat. Adding full power at the last second at least avoided the crash and instead got me into an early wire and most importantly taught me a critical lesson about flying around the carrier at night.

So many aspects about landing on an aircraft carrier are counterintuitive to new pilots. First, you basically fly the airplane backward in the sense that your stick doesn't control your altitude but rather your attitude (fast versus slow essentially), and your throttle doesn't control your speed but rather your descent rate and subsequent glideslope. Those aspects can be practiced at a normal runway during the instructional flights prior to being at the aircraft carrier. What can't be practiced in advance is what the winds will do to you when you're lined up to land behind the boat.

For starters, the carrier flight deck is 60 feet above the waterline and the landing area is angled about 10 degrees from the direction the ship moves. What that means in practice is that your runway is routinely shifting to the right. That challenge is usually easier to manage than the challenge of the winds because you can at least see the landing area, whereas you can't see the wind. Our airplanes work best with about 20 knots of wind over the landing area, which is easily accomplished by having the ship go 20 knots (on a calm day) or having it pointed into the direction of the wind, assuming the sea space we're operating in allows for that. The challenge begins when the wind passes over the flight deck and then drops down 60 feet and bounces off the water. The way it affects us when we're landing is that wind, after crossing the flight deck and bouncing off the water, usually gets to us about 5–10 seconds before touchdown, and the typical effect is that it pushes us up higher than we want to be. The natural reaction then is to pull the power back to allow the aircraft to descend, but as soon as that input takes effect the plane is through that area of rising wind and now in the area with no wind at all because the superstructure is blocking it and the rest of it is below you bouncing off the water. That causes the airplane to seemingly fall out of the sky and you've just exacerbated that problem by reducing the power.

It's this challenge that routinely causes our nugget pilots to get behind the jet and come careening down toward the back of the boat. With enough experience you eventually learn to add power at a certain point to counteract this problem, but it's not necessarily intuitive, certainly not early on in your career. On that particular night, I was overconfident and complacent, certainly for my total lack of experience flying behind the boat at night. Because of that, I fell victim to one of the pitfalls of carrier landings, and were it not for the quick reaction of our LSO, I'd likely not be here telling the story.

That, however, wasn't my first failure in aviation. As I look back on my twenty-plus years of flying for the Navy, I'm grateful for the opportunities and experiences. It was far more exciting and fulfilling than I ever anticipated; however, my career in aviation started as a failure and it somehow went downhill from there.

Somewhere around the age of thirteen, I decided I wanted to join the military. For me this was very much connected to the Gulf War and our country's support for the men and women heading off to faraway places to fight for us. Furthermore, I decided around the same time that I wanted to be a Navy SEAL. This was around 1990–91, and back then the SEALs were not as well known as they are today, after decades of attention for their heroic operations around the world following 9/11. In my family, and even among my closest friends, going to college wasn't an option to be decided on; it was expected, so the idea of enlisting never even occurred to me. College was the way.

I decided the most logical route to becoming a Navy SEAL and attending college was to attend the U.S. Naval Academy in Annapolis, Maryland. It provided a college education that was not only free but paid its students each month (not a whole lot, though), and each of the graduates were automatically commissioned into the U.S. Navy. At that time each class graduated only sixteen future SEALs, but I felt like that was the best option.

So at the young age of thirteen I became singularly focused on getting accepted into the Naval Academy and prepared myself as best I could to be the ideal applicant. The various service academies are generally looking for well-rounded applicants rather than young men and women who are narrowly focused on either academics or sports. They are looking for applicants who have good (not necessarily perfect) test scores, have good grades, participate if not lead their high school sports teams, are part of civic organizations, and so on. I did what I thought was required and was overjoyed when I was accepted into the Naval Academy's Class of 2000, and off I went in the summer of '96 to join my classmates as we began our journey to eventually become officers in the U.S. Navy.

I took the same approach to becoming a SEAL as I had to gaining admission to the Naval Academy: I studied what aspects were most important and tried to focus my efforts on excelling in those areas. SEALs are expected to be on the extreme upper levels of physical fitness and exceptionally strong in the water, so I spent my days in the pool and exercising in addition to trying to maintain a high class rank to better distinguish myself from the hundreds of other SEAL "wannabes."

Despite four years of focused effort, on the night our service selections were announced I was assigned Navy pilot, which had been my second choice. Crushed and devastated, I wept uncontrollably, not for minutes but for days. For me it was the fact that I had spent what felt like my entire life singularly focused on one particular goal. In my mind, I'd done all I could to accomplish that goal, and for someone who'd been successful in all my major endeavors to that point, this marked a failure in magnitude I struggled to comprehend. Worse still was the reality that I couldn't just keep trying—the door to the Navy SEALs was closed forever.

When we go to flight school in the Navy, it's a long, arduous process. It takes every bit of two full years and costs the government millions of dollars per pilot. Because of that, the service requirement following flight school is different than for the other warfare specialties. For example, someone who chooses to be a surface warfare officer and serves onboard a ship or someone who becomes a submarine officer and serves onboard a nuclear-powered submarine owes five years of service after graduating from the Naval Academy. The same service requirement applies to graduates who went into the Marine Corps and the SEAL teams. For aviation, however, because of the expense and amount of training, we owe eight years following our winging ceremony, so usually about ten years total time in service. That's a long way of explaining why I wouldn't be able to go to flight school, learn to fly airplanes, graduate and get winged, then decide I wanted to transition and apply again to the Navy SEALs. It just was not in the cards.

So that night of service assignment, it was clear to me that my dream of becoming a Navy SEAL, everything I'd focused on and worked toward for almost ten years, was over. I couldn't appeal the decision; I couldn't ask to be reconsidered. It was done and final. After I was able to get past my immediate disappointment, the next order of business was giving up my hobbies that I enjoyed so much and thought would be best preparing me to serve in the SEALs: skydiving, scuba diving, and rock climbing. Those were done, at least for the time, and my focus had to be on flying airplanes, not jumping out of them.

After a great deal of introspection and advice from mentors, I slowly came to the realization that up to that point, I had made it about me. I wanted to serve in a specific capacity as a Navy SEAL. I felt it would bring me the most pleasure and satisfaction and that I would be able to contribute to the defense of our country most effectively in that position. Two notable points on that topic were that this was the winter of 1999–2000 and our country was at a very different point militarily then than we were a short year and a half later when we were attacked. Next and more importantly, everything I just explained there started with either a "me" or an "I," and yet it still wasn't apparent to me that I was making it about me rather than my service.

I don't believe many, if any, people join the military because they want to be famous or rich. If they did, they were sadly misled. I certainly didn't join under any false pretenses; I joined because, as I said before, I felt truly called to serve. Despite the service assignment not being what I wanted, that aspect of me hadn't changed. So it was then at the young age of twenty-two that it finally dawned on me that it wasn't *how* I served; it was simply *that* I served. It didn't matter how I gave of my time and talent for my country's defense; it just mattered that I gave of myself for a great cause.

I didn't want to have to learn that lesson—I wanted to be a SEAL. It was a blessing in disguise: my failure taught me a lesson that proved crucial for my maturation and, I believe, for my growth as an individual. It was also the first time I had failed, *really* failed hard. Failed in such a way that it couldn't be glossed over or hidden. Failed in such a way that I had to go on almost a calling spree to let everyone I was close to know that I'd failed. I told my parents almost right away, through my tears and confusion. The hard part was the days that followed as my lifetime friends checked in to see what had happened. I had to go through with them each how I'd failed in my goal, in my chosen profession. It was a miserable time to be me, but I think with each conversation, with each spoken admission of my failure, a little fire began to burn that would eventually lead to successes that far exceeded my then failure.

I was twenty-two when I was first introduced to the benefit of failure. At that point, with reflection and self-analysis, I was able to reorient my life through my thoughts and my goals. I was able to make my service to my country more selfless than selfish. It was at that point that I decided I was going to head down to flight school and outwork every single person who was down there. I was preparing to compete with thousands of men and women who hadn't failed—they had succeeded in getting their first choice, their lifetime dream was coming true to be Navy pilots. Many of them had already spent years flying; some were not just licensed but had been flight instructors and had thousands of flight hours already in their logbook. Others had majored in aerospace engineering, and while I was doing math proofs and Calculus 8, they were designing aircraft in labs. At that point I couldn't have told you what the difference was between lift and drag, and some of them were off to get master's degrees as aerospace engineers. That was my competition, and it didn't look good from where I sat.

Nonetheless, a goal is a goal, and my goal then was to outwork them all despite how excited and motivated they each were. My reasoning at the time was simply that I didn't even want to be there. I wanted to be in Coronado, California, going through BUD/S, the SEAL training pipeline, but instead I was in Pensacola, Florida, taking courses on aerodynamics and meteorology. My mindset became that it would say more about me, the person I was, and more importantly, it would say more about my service if I outworked the people who wanted to be there when I was still depressed at having failed. That mindset change for me was almost a mental rebirth. It opened me up to the idea of selfless service, and I found that I had more energy, more motivation, and was even more capable when I was doing something because it was the right thing to do rather than what I wanted to do. So with my head down and focused on the mission ahead, I set off to be the best flight school student in the history of the Navy.

It didn't take very long for me to prove to myself and the Navy that I was far from that. Worse still, I was rapidly approaching the position of being the worst flight school student in the Navy. Flight school starts with API, Aviation Preflight Indoctrination. It's not long, only six weeks, and the first four weeks were primarily classes and coursework, followed by aviation-specific survival portions, like water survival, pressure chambers, parachute landings, and so on. The classroom portion was first a few weeks of aerodynamics, learning why planes were able to fly, what equations enabled aircraft design, and so on. We also took courses on weather, navigation, engines, and physiology. We were tested on each subject, and an 80 percent was considered a passing grade. Your overall grade would be included with your grades from actual flights when it came time to select what type of aircraft you flew, so everyone was quite motivated to excel. I did fine in the first few subjects, but the engineering test, called engines at the time, wasn't my best subject. In fact, it didn't seem to make sense at all, and despite my attempts at rote memorization, I took the test and received a 78. I was pulled aside at the end of the day, a Friday, and told I had failed the test and would retake it on Monday morning. That weekend was particularly tough for me as my father had been having medical complications from a long-term illness, and I was planning to go home to Atlanta from Pensacola to spend the weekend with my parents. I did in fact do that and returned late Sunday night. I went in an hour before our classes started on Monday to retake my engines exam. They graded it right away and told me I'd gotten a 76.

I was immediately pulled out of my class and dropped from the group of students I'd been going through API with. They'd all passed the test and were moving into the next level of instruction, but I wasn't going with them. I waited for what seemed like forever to be seen by the Navy captain who was the head of the aviation school's command. Eventually I was ushered into his office and was subsequently berated by him for my poor performance. It started with him opening a file that had my grades from the Naval Academy. I had been a decent student, graduated in the top 10 percent in the somewhat difficult major of mathematics, and he had those grades. He was able to see that I'd received almost exclusively A's in all my engineering courses and wasn't shy about mentioning that. Ultimately the point he made was that clearly I didn't care, I wasn't trying, and I must not want to be there—that was the only explanation for my substandard performance. Although I felt differently, I wasn't in a great position to argue or defend my case.

He then went on to say that we each get three strikes and I'd used two of them. He also added that he was changing the rules for me given my grades from the Academy that he was looking at. I would retake the engines exam and the two other exams I had remaining (navigation, and flight rules and regulations), and if I didn't make at least a 94 on all of them, I would be removed from the aviation pipeline and would be transitioned to some other warfare specialty elsewhere in the Navy. I had two days to prepare. I would take the engines exam again, and if I passed it, I would be rolled into the class that was a week behind my original class; and if I didn't, I would be out the door.

Clearly, as I'm writing this chapter after having spent my career flying F/A-18s, I passed the engines exam along with the other two. I'm not sure exactly what I did differently; I felt like I'd given all I could the first time around. If it taught me anything, it's that you always have a bit more to give. It also taught me a critical lesson that served me well my entire career, and that was that there's always another way. If what you're doing isn't working, it doesn't mean you're not able to succeed. You just need to try another method. One of my absolute favorite quotes about failure (of which there are many!) is from Henry Ford. He said, "Failure is simply the opportunity to begin again, this time more intelligently." That rang true for me at the time. I had failed very early on in my flight school career, so I could either hang it up, say it's just not for me, or I could pick up the pieces and start again, more intelligently. Thankfully, I decided on the second option because I have loved nearly every minute of my career flying airplanes.

I would love to say the engines test marked the end of my failure story, but that was not the case. I finished API and moved about thirty minutes north to Milton, Florida, the home of NAS Whiting Field, where about half of the Navy's pilots go to learn how to actually fly. In those days, there was no introductory flight training, so for many of us, our first time flying an airplane was when we strapped into the seat of the then T-34C, the Turbo Mentor. It was a two-seat, tandem-style plane with the student up front and the instructor directly behind. It had a turboprop engine, which meant it was far more powerful than a traditional turbine engine—it was in fact a jet engine powering a propeller. That meant it could fly extremely fast for a prop plane and do an impressive amount of aerobatics and formation flying. We were in Whiting Field to learn all those things and, based on our performance, we would select our future aircraft type, meaning jets, helicopters, maritime, and so on.

We each sat through a few weeks of ground school to learn the airplane, its systems, and its EPs, and once we were taught and tested, we were sent to our respective squadrons to learn how to fly. My instructor was then-Lt. Brad Davis, a helicopter pilot who had excelled in his fleet squadron and was back to teach us how to fly in the T-34C. We were his first students, and he had a great deal of energy and enthusiasm for training us. Sadly for me, I was the opposite of a naturally gifted aviator; I was a fledging buffoon, and that's probably even a bit generous. On my first scheduled training flight, my ability to taxi it correctly—that is, drive it around on the ground—was so bad that they had to schedule me for additional training, remedial taxi training. Imagine explaining that one to your buddies when they see an odd line on the flight schedule for the day. "Hey, what are you doing? What's that 'taxi fam' mean on the schedule?" It's more than a little embarrassing, and I suspect each of them took pleasure in knowing they wouldn't have to work very hard to outperform me.

Once I had figured out how to taxi, they actually let me take off and fly. On our very first flight, the instructor would usually conduct the takeoff from the back. If memory serves me, the instructor would tell you that you get to take off. He'd also say that you're going to hold the brakes, add up the power, watch your legs shake, release the brakes, not add enough rudder, swerve violently from side to side, modulate the throttle for no reason at all, and then he would stop the entire evolution and take off from the back. So, yep, that's exactly what happened.

Nonetheless, within seconds of being airborne and being at the controls of the T-34C, I fell fully in love with aviation.

Regrettably for me, being in love with aviation wasn't enough to be good at aviation. I worked through my introductory flights, learning the basics of how to take off and land, how to talk on the radio and navigate, even what to do when certain emergencies occurred. The syllabus allowed for about a dozen flights, and then each student had a "Safe for Solo" check ride. The flight was exactly what it sounded like: it was our first check ride and was intended to determine if we were safe to fly the airplane alone and without an instructor. The critical components were can you take off and land safely, can you get to where you're going and make it back to the original location, and can you demonstrate that you know what to do if something goes wrong? Sounds simple enough, but some of those things are harder than you might imagine and not everyone excels at this check ride. I certainly didn't.

I was able to demonstrate an ability to talk on the radios, navigate, and safely handle the airplane if the engine quit. What I didn't excel at was landing and as such failed the check ride. I was told I'd have the chance to try it again and was offered one remedial flight with a different instructor to work on landing techniques. However, should I fail the check ride on the next flight, my time in flight school was finished. This is a trickier problem than some of the earlier failures because there's no way to practice landing an airplane without being in an airplane. All the studying in the world won't make you any better, so there's very little you can do in that situation aside from hope and pray you do better the next time around.

Once again, I wouldn't be writing this chapter had I failed that check ride, but suffice it to say, I wasn't a natural aviator and landings were never necessarily my strong suit. Also of import, Navy pilots aren't known for their soft or "greased on" landings, so perhaps in the back of my mind I didn't really care all that much. Either way, I survived the check ride, but the failure that led to it played a crucial role in my journey as a Navy pilot.

I don't love spending so much time talking about all the ways I failed so early on in my career. I don't view it as being therapeutic or liberating. What I do know is that it shaped who I am as a person and as a naval officer. It also propelled me forward in a way that, I think, success in any or all of those endeavors wouldn't have done. The failures taught me a new way of approaching problems. They taught me that if the first way I attacked an issue didn't work, it wasn't necessarily that I couldn't do it or it was impossible to accomplish; it just meant I needed to try something else. As simple as that sounds, it can be complicated to understand for some people. That sentiment is stated much more succinctly by Thomas Edison, who wrote, "I have not failed. I've just found 10,000 ways that won't work."

The individuals I've met along the way who seem to suffer the most damage from failure, as counterintuitive as this might be, are those who have never failed. You might naturally think that people who fail constantly finally get fed up with failing and ultimately just give up, but that's not been my experience—quite the opposite in fact. Those folks tend to be the most resilient and are often the most creative in their approach to solving problems.

The people that failure seems to conquer the easiest are often the most capable. It's the individuals who have never failed before, and when it finally happens, that failure finds them totally helpless and with no ability to move past it. A perfect example of that sort of person is a student at one of our country's service academies. This is a group of young men and women who have largely been successful in everything they've tried up to that point. By virtue of the admissions process as I mentioned before, the service academies seek out applicants who are well rounded rather than being extremely strong in just one aspect. They seek out students with great grades, not perfect grades, high SAT/ACT scores, not 1600s, and they look for captains of their sports teams and leaders of their clubs and community service groups. These are students who have competed and excelled and been recognized for it. When you spend your life excelling and winning, it makes losing much harder; you're not accustomed to it, and you're not good at it.

I firmly believe that those who are most successful are those who have failed. A favorite section of a speech made by Theodore Roosevelt titled "Citizenship in a Republic," given in Paris in 1910, is often required to be memorized by new students at the Naval Academy. The entire speech is quite long, but the section most often learned is referred to as the "Man in the Arena," and this is it:

> It is not the critic who counts; not the man who points out how the strong man stumbles, or where the doer of

> deeds could have done them better. The credit belongs to the man who is actually in the arena, whose face is marred by dust and sweat and blood; who strives valiantly; who errs, who comes short again and again, because there is no effort without error and shortcoming; but who does actually strive to do the deeds; who knows the great enthusiasms, the great devotions; who spends himself in a worthy cause; who at the best knows in the end the triumph of high achievement, and who at the worst, if he fails, at least fails while daring greatly, so that his place shall never be with those cold and timid souls who neither know victory nor defeat.

That passage is so incredibly motivating for so many. It reassures us that it's okay to fail; it encourages us to try and try again. Still though, the idea or the possibility of failure can be so daunting to many of us that it's not worth trying. When I was still in my first squadron, my commanding officer recommended that I apply to the Blue Angels. My career timing was nonstandard due to my time as a flight instructor in Meridian, and as such, it was going to perhaps cause some challenges for me on my fitness reports (FITREPs) as I became more senior. The Navy's FITREP system certainly isn't perfect, but we use it as best we can to identify who is best suited for promotion and subsequent commands. Trusting him and taking his advice, I looked closer into the Blue Angels and what it would take to apply. Up until that point, I had fully intended to apply either to TOPGUN or to test pilot school (TPS) because I believed they would offer the most challenge and position me well to be successful in the naval aviation enterprise.

At that time, I had no experience with or knowledge of the Blue Angels in any way aside from having watched them a time or two at air shows when I had taken a jet to be used as a static display. I made what I figured was a normal assumption that the pilots were cocky and arrogant and flew like cowboys. It's not a smart business practice to blow off the recommendation of your commanding officer, so I sent in the correct forms and asked to be considered as an applicant to the Blue Angels in the spring of 2007. Applicants are expected to spend time with the team, and that's accomplished by them attending a few air shows in the spring of that year. They're expected to attend the flight brief prior to the air show and then also spend the evenings socializing with the officers and meeting our sailors. The intent is for the Blue Angels to get to know the applicant personally, see if they are someone we can spend a great deal of time with, and see if they're able to proudly represent the Navy and Marine Corps.

Because of my (thankfully incorrect) assumptions, I wasn't looking forward to the time with the team and figured it would be a lot of me kissing the ring and sucking up. I felt so strongly that this would be the case that I bought my wife a commercial ticket to join me at the air show, which is a huge no-no for the applicants because their time is meant to be spent with the team. I was hedging my bets in a way, assuming I wouldn't care for them, wouldn't enjoy the experience in general, and then would gracefully decline to participate any further and enjoy a weekend at the beach with my wife.

I walked into the area near the briefing room and was immediately greeted by the team's flight surgeon, Mark

Lambert. Mark was a lieutenant commander at the time, a Naval Academy graduate, and subsequently a graduate of Georgetown University School of Medicine. He introduced himself, asked me about myself and my family, and was about as gracious a person as I'd ever met. Mark was followed by a handful of other Blue Angels who all came out, introduced themselves, then proceeded to make a genuine effort to get to know me. I was floored. I truly couldn't hide my surprise and wasn't sure if I was being punked somehow. There was no groveling, kissing the ring, anything remotely resembling that; instead it was an opportunity to meet some fantastic men and women. When I finally saw my wife much later that evening, having spent the rest of the day and night with the team, I couldn't help but share my surprise and excitement. I told her that I was sure I wouldn't be chosen, but regardless I'd met some incredible people, and I was better just for having gotten to know them.

I was further impressed over the next few months as I spent a few more weekends with them, watching their show and getting to know them better. My assumption about them being cowboys couldn't have been further from the truth. Instead, it was unquestionably the most professional group of Navy and Marine officers I'd ever met, and their love for service was only eclipsed by the degree to which they took flying a safe and professional air show. Their expectations were high and their tolerance for mistakes was incredibly low, and they held themselves to a standard I hadn't before witnessed.

I knew practically right away it was the job I wanted to do. I hadn't wanted anything that much in my life, not even to be a Navy SEAL.

I share this with you because something else extraordinary happened when I returned from my first air show weekend. A number of the other junior officers started asking me questions about how it went and what the process was like. It turned out they knew far more than I did about the Blue Angels. It was quite remarkable recounting what had happened and then being asked very specific questions about certain activities and experiences. I asked them how they had any idea about what took place, and the answers varied from "I watched their documentary" to "I've read every book there is about them" and so on. It slowly dawned on me that each of them very much wanted to be on the "Blues," yet they hadn't applied. Here I was, thinking I didn't even want to do it, and I'd thrown my hat in the ring. The sad thought that occurred to me was that they hadn't done the same because despite how much they wanted the job, they were too scared of failure, too scared of not being selected.

It reminded me of yet another quote from Theodore Roosevelt: "It is hard to fail, but it is worse never to have tried to succeed." I felt bad for them; I was sad to realize that they were too afraid of failure to pursue a dream. That was the gift I'd received from my many failures, certainly in aviation. I wasn't afraid to fail. It wasn't a consideration at all. It wasn't that I was numb to it, but rather I'd learned the hard lesson of recognizing failure not as a negative but as an opportunity. I knew I was better for having failed.

There's nothing hard about the "Man in the Arena" passage or my Blue Angel applicant example to understand. In practice, though, it's very hard to do. When failure occurs, those words don't always seem to apply. Whereas before they made perfect sense, once you're face-to-face with your own personal failures, it becomes easy to say, "Well, those words don't cover this particular case," or maybe, "My situation is clearly different." The hard part about failure is recognizing it for what it is and then using what you knew to be the case, knew to be the right response, and seeing it through.

Very few, if any, would advocate for quitting at the first hint of failure. Almost everyone would insist that is the precise time to step it up. Yet so many find themselves unable to do so. So many think in that moment that their failure is somehow unique and even perhaps worse than others'.

I love using or referencing the analogy of testing a new aircraft. Anytime our engineers design a new plane, it goes through years of testing. We have progressed so incredibly far in our approach that a great deal of the testing can now be done on a computer, in laboratories, even in wind tunnels with scaled models of the new airplane. What this does is make the job of the test pilots much, *much* safer. In the early days of aviation, being a test pilot was akin to being a polar explorer. It took experience, courage, and a good deal of luck, or maybe better stated, good fortune. A great deal of our success in that sort of endeavor lies in luck, or things outside of our control.

Once the airplane is designed, engineered, and built, it's ready for its first test flight. These flights are usually as basic as it gets. The aircraft lifts off, doesn't raise its gear, turns downwind, and then lands. This of course happens only after it conducts high-speed taxi trials and so on, in a crawl, walk, run approach. As the airplane continues to perform according to expectations, it continues to be tested with more and more rigor and eventually more and more aggressiveness.

When the airplane is eventually mass produced and arrives in the various squadrons, it is accompanied with a large manual that explains every aspect about it. It covers each and every system and how they work in unison with one another, and it covers the aircraft's limitations. It might be something as simple as a speed limit—for example, this aircraft is not to exceed 1.8 M (or 1.8 x Mach [the speed of sound]). It also might be more specific, such as no rolling maneuvers are allowed with the gear extended that exceed 1.5 Gs. The limitations are numerous and varied, and they exist because some brave test pilot was willing to push the aircraft until the point it failed.

When the airplane was being tested, long before it found itself in the hands of the squadron pilots, those test pilots flew the pants off that plane. They put it in situations that you'd never deliberately put an airplane, just to see how it performed. They endeavored to do almost everything stupid that can be done just to see the aircraft's flying performance and to ascertain if any unexpected anomalies existed. While I was working side by side with the test pilots at our base in Pax River, Maryland, one engineer remarked when answering a question, "Never underestimate a pilot's ability to eff something up that you didn't anticipate." It was said sort of tongue-in-cheek, but it was basically serious, and it spoke to the rigor they apply as engineers designing new aircraft and the associated aircraft systems. They can't build it to fly in only perfect scenarios; they build it to fly in the worst scenarios. For our fighters, they have to design them to fly after they've been shot and lost portions of their flight controls. In fact, the aircraft are designed to such an incredible degree that on one beautiful sunny day while I was a part of a photo shoot, there was an airborne collision, a mishap where one aircraft hit another and the stabilator off one Hornet was ripped off. About one half of the entire flight control surface—that is, the surface that allows the aircraft to both climb and turn—was broken off and fell into the ocean below. Our aircraft is a fly-by-wire airplane, which means its flight controls work in conjunction with one another and adjust as required when necessary. In this case, half of the stab was gone, and the airplane didn't alert the pilot in any way. We have an entire display on our screens just for flight controls to show us how each surface is functioning, and it didn't display a single error, or X as we refer to the portions of the system that aren't functioning normally. If almost any other normal aircraft lost that sizable a portion of its control surfaces, it would have been rendered unflyable and would have likely departed controlled flight and been unrecoverable. Our aircraft was basically saying, "I'm fine. I've got this."

The point is, they're extremely well-designed airplanes, and they are that way because of the experience and expertise of some very bright engineers. The test pilots still put them through the paces in an attempt to determine the aircraft's fight envelope, which is its limit of capability. We refer to that envelope regularly, and if we do something dangerous, it's likely "outside the envelope," which is a place you don't want to be.

I use that explanation because we as humans are very similar to aircraft in that it's largely unknown what we're capable of until we're tested. When we test ourselves, when we're tested by our jobs, our friends, our experiences, it's only then that we're able to determine what we're capable of. It's after we get put through the paces that we're able to determine our own personal envelope.

What my analogy doesn't perfectly encapsulate is the fact that no matter how great our airplanes are, we are better. Our envelope isn't fixed; it isn't final. Our envelope can be expanded when we learn from our failures. "Failure is success in progress," said a wise man known as Albert Einstein. When we test our personal envelope and find its limits, we might view them as failures, and sure that's a fair assessment. But if we're able to pick ourselves up and move on more intelligently, then perhaps that envelope shifts with us. Perhaps that failure isn't failure at all; it's just success in progress. It doesn't change the fact that to even know your own personal envelope at all you have to be willing to test it, and to do that you have to be willing to fail.

I mentioned before that the students at the service academies were uniquely positioned to be caught off guard by failing. I've had the privilege of speaking to groups of them over the years, and I very much like to make the point that when they fail, I think it's critical for them to look at their mentors or those whom they respect and look up to. I tell them that I believe that while they're probably respected for their successes, what's not seen is their failures. I think that sentiment is true for all of us, regardless of our lot in life, our profession, our background, or whatever our differences may be. When we see people whom we believe to be massive successes, we don't see the fact that they might consider themselves failures. They might think they've failed more than most, but what they didn't do was stay down. They picked themselves up and moved on more intelligently and stronger for having failed. I would submit that one thing all highly successful people have in common is that they're not only willing to fail but that they're motivated by failure and the lessons they learn through it. Michael Jordan famously said, "I've missed more than 9,000 shots in my career. I've lost almost 300 games. Twenty-six times, I've been trusted to take the game-winning shot and missed. I've failed over and over and over again in my life. And that is why I succeed."

As Navy pilots, one of the unique aspects of our job is landing aboard an aircraft carrier. I've explained it at length in the first chapter, but what I didn't mention is that every landing is not only watched by nearly the entire ship on closed-circuit TVs; they're also each graded. The grades are given by a team of pilots known as LSOs, and their job is to safely recover aircraft while at sea. In most squadrons, it's an honor to be chosen to be an LSO. Because the LSOs are responsible for the safe recovery and the grades, they must have a level of respect as pilots in order to be able to properly debrief the other pilots on their approaches and landings. Another added benefit is that the LSOs are removed from the traditional duty or watch schedule, and therefore their nonflying time is spent on the flight deck recovering aircraft rather than down below managing the daily flight schedule from behind a desk. In short, it's a great opportunity with a lot of responsibility for a junior officer to have and enjoy.

Landing jets, or any planes, on a moving ship is, as you might expect, challenging and it takes a lot of separate people and actions happening correctly and in sequence for it to work properly. It's not simply enough for the pilot at the controls to fly a nice approach. If the ship isn't navigating correctly, especially in areas of challenging sea space, then it's all for naught. If the men and women responsible for setting the proper tension on the arresting gear, which varies for every landing based on the weight of the plane, then the pilot is either unable to land at all or to land safely. It takes the flight deck personnel to get each aircraft out of the landing area and taxied into its new position in less than forty-five seconds to ensure the next aircraft can safely land. In short, it takes the entire ship working in perfect harmony to launch and recover airplanes.

Because of all that, carrier landings are known to carry additional risk and have a higher degree of mishaps associated with them, or at least they certainly did for a long time. Years ago, in an effort to increase the percentage of safe landings, an idea arose to grade landings and then to make the pilots compete for grades. It was one of those genius ideas that makes everyone wonder why it took so long to figure out in the first place. As it turns out, most of the pilots very much had type-A personalities and the idea of new competition was exciting and welcomed. The time on a deployment was then broken up into separate periods, much like trimesters, and the grades were tracked and tallied, and those with the best grades not only got recognized for it in front of the entire air wing, but they were given patches to proudly display on their flight jackets. Pilots who routinely were in the top ten had their jackets adorned in patches up their sleeves, and it would command the respect of their fellow air crew with the instant credibility that came with the recognition.

The landings were graded on a 4.0 scale with an above-average landing being given a 4.0. It was referred to as "OK," which is a testament to the type of people we're dealing with; there's always room for improvement when the best you can do is just "OK." If the landing was considered safe but had deviations on the approach that were outside of the briefed tolerance (i.e., too high, too low, or unnecessarily fast or slow), then the landing was called "Fair" and given a 3.0. If the pilot landed short and arrived in the first wire, that was generally graded as a "No Grade" and given a 2.0. Landing in the first wire would intuitively be the best, but in fact it means you were so far below glideslope that much lower and you wouldn't have landed at all but instead ended up firmly implanted into the back of the ship. If the pilot missed all the wires, it was called a "Bolter" and graded as a 2.5. Then there was a 1.0 for a "Waveoff" when the LSOs thought you were so far outside of the safe recovery envelope that they called for you to go around, and the absolute worst was a "Cut Pass" and graded as a 0.0. That landing would get you the attention of all the LSOs and perhaps even the CAG (Commander Air Group—the most senior officer in a carrier air wing). That was generally reserved for something so unsafe that it could and possibly even should have cost you your life or the loss of the plane. Thankfully those passes were *very* few and far between.

Normally the LSOs were able to safely recover the planes and use the grading system to teach the pilots how to land better. Keep in mind that this entire graded portion of the landing is only the last 15–18 seconds, but a lot can happen in that short time. In the space of that 15 seconds, we break it down into distinct portions: "the start" (the first few seconds), "in the middle" (the next few seconds), "in close" (the last few seconds), and then "at the ramp," which refers to when the plane is over the carrier deck but still descending to the point of touchdown where the arresting cable is. For example, here's a possible landing grade: H.X NEP.CDIM LIC-AR: Fair 2 wire. What that means is that the aircraft started too high, hence the High Start (H.X). Then the pilot didn't add enough power in the middle of the approach, hence the Not Enough Power on the Come Down in the Middle. Because of that poor correction of not adding enough power, the pilot found him- or herself low from "in close" to "at the ramp," hence the LIC-AR. Because of the magnitude of the deviations, the grade is not "OK" but rather "Fair," and they ended up in the 2 wire. This sort of pass would no doubt disappoint the pilot, but learning takes place when he or she reviews the landing both on the TV display and the tapes from the heads-up display and tries to identify what went wrong. They know from the grade that they started off too high, so they can go backward and see what part of the approach caused that, and then furthermore they can figure out why they took off so much power allowing them to settle and go low. This sort of debrief becomes their "what not to do" on the next flight plan. Over many landings and debriefs, the pilots get better and safer.

Most pilots work very hard to have only OK passes, and even an occasional Fair pass would set them off and likely eliminate them from contention for the top ten. There were very rare cases where the pilot would come around the turn perhaps higher or lower than was acceptable for the OK pass tolerance, but through some mystery known only to the naval aviation gods, the pilot would end up back in a perfect position, on altitude, airspeed, and lineup and would proceed to execute a flawless last few seconds through touchdown. This sort of thing, as I said, happened very infrequently, but when it did, it sort of left the LSOs rubbing their chins and pondering what they'd seen.

When a pilot pulled off something like this, their grade might read: H.X NC (HIC-AR): OK 3 wire. In English that is High Start followed by a Nice Correction, and then just a little bit high "in close" until touchdown on the flight deck ("at the ramp"). OK pass into the 3 wire. In short, the LSO is stating that the pilot was too high at the start and normally would get an automatic Fair pass for that deviation. However, the correction made was so incredible or eye-watering that it was given the comment "Nice Correction," and it became upgraded to an OK pass. Much like the best you can do is OK, I always joked that the "once-in-a-blue-moon" almost unheard-of comment for incredible airmanship was simply "Nice."

I go through this long explanation to ensure you appreciate the significance of it. As I said, for us out at sea and landing on a moving ship, it doesn't happen often. What it did teach me is that we're each able to make a Nice Correction. We will fail; that's an absolute certainty. We will falter, we will fall down, we will find ourselves thinking we've done something unrecoverable. At our absolute lowest in that moment, we find ourselves thinking we'll never be able to fix the failure. That's the time when it's absolutely critical to remember that we're each capable of making a Nice Correction. We have it in us and if we execute it correctly, those around us will be left shaking their heads and pondering how we pulled it off.

The idea of a Nice Correction certainly applies outside of naval aviation. Regardless of whether your failure happens at work, in a relationship, or elsewhere, there's always an opportunity for a Nice Correction. What I've found that works best for me is taking deliberate time to think about the failure. When something goes wrong, regardless of where it falls on the failure spectrum, you can move on and try to forget it happened or to some degree dwell on it. Normally dwelling on a mistake doesn't sound like the right response, but I would offer that if the intent of dwelling on it is to correct it in some way and then learn from it to prevent it from happening again, then it's absolutely the right plan. I'd further suggest that if dwelling on it somehow allows you to arrive at a course of action that enables a Nice Correction and leaves those around you wondering how you took a mistake and managed to turn it into a net benefit, then it's definitely the way to go.

Anytime I've had the opportunity to mentor a junior officer, a sailor, a friend, or even one of my children, that's my constant refrain. I share with them how we all fail, we all screw up, constantly even. What separates the good from the great is the willingness to put deliberate time, effort, and thought into learning from it and then trying to arrive at a place where you are better for having made the mistake. When you get to that point you know you're succeeding because of failure, and your opportunities for success have just risen significantly and substantially.

CHAPTER 7

COURAGE

"Courage is found in unlikely places."

—J. R. R. TOLKIEN

"Boss, Kitty. My right gen [generator] is inop [inoperative]. I tried a reset, no joy." Those words were spoken by USMC Maj. Chris "Kitty" Collins, Blue Angel #4 (our Slot pilot), to our commanding officer and flight leader, Blue Angel #1, Greg McWherter. It took place almost exactly 1,100 nm after takeoff from Travis Air Force Base in Fairfield, California, as we were en route to MCAS (Marine Corps Air Station) Hawai'i in Kaneohe Bay. That distance, 1,100 nm, was incredibly important because the entire trip was 2,200 nm, and there were no land or runways—in fact there was nothing between the coast of California and the coast of Hawai'i.

We flew that route, seven total Blue Angel F/A-18s, led by two KC-135 USAF tankers who provided us aerial refueling along the route because our planes carried only enough fuel to transit roughly 800 nm. That meant there was quite a large area over the Pacific Ocean that if something went wrong, we wouldn't have enough fuel to make it to land. It's also important to point out that there are a lot of sharks, really big sharks, in the Pacific Ocean, and that's generally the first thing that comes to mind when you realize you don't have enough fuel to make it to land.

The USAF tankers were managed as a Coronet mission, meaning a specific mission designed to get fighters across either the Atlantic or the Pacific Ocean. As such, the mission was briefed by the USAF and the products (our flight plans, waypoints, frequencies, kneeboard cars, etc.) were all provided by them. Furthermore, they set the ground rules—they decided the takeoff time, the route, the mission abort criteria. They controlled everything except telling us how to fly our respective airplanes. As such, it was their brief and plan that should any emergency arise prior to getting halfway across the Pacific, we would be required to perform an immediate 180 and return to Travis AFB. This of course brought with it a slew of other problems. We'd kept a small crew of some of our best maintainers at Travis should something happen, but our access to parts was limited because they didn't have any F/A-18s based there and it's impossible to plan for every possible contingency. Additionally, we had an air show to fly in Hawai'i that weekend, so any planes that returned to Travis would have to eventually make the flight out there and go through the same lengthy process with Coronet in hopes of it being successful on the next attempt.

Short story now made long: it couldn't have happened at a worse time.

The problem with having a generator go offline is that it provides half the power to the plane. The plane can operate on a single generator, but it bears twice the load and there's no telling how long it will operate, especially without knowing why the first one went offline unexpectedly. If you lose both generators, life gets bad exceedingly fast. The airplane is then running on battery power, and there's very little of it to use. That far away from land, it's basically a foregone conclusion that you won't be able to make it to land without at least one operating generator. We all knew that; it didn't have to be said aloud.

After Kitty reported the malfunction to Boss, our flight leader, there was a momentary pause, perhaps five seconds—although to all of us flying our respective planes, holding our collective breath, it seemed like an eternity. Boss came back as calm and collected as I've ever heard anyone to this day talk on the radio: "Okay, Kitty, here's the plan. If the left gen cuts off, I want you to separate from the formation and fly at a safe distance below us. Turn off everything: your radios, your displays, and pull your FCS [flight control system] circuit breakers. When you know you're ready to get fuel, reset your FCS circuit breakers and we'll clear out so you can get gas as quickly and efficiently as possible. As soon as you're topped off, pull the circuit breaker and do your best to stay below us. If you have to get out of the plane, do your absolute best to find a ship and eject alongside or in their vicinity. We'll do our best to get assets heading your way immediately."

"Got it, Boss. Understood," Kitty replied.

It's not exceptionally hard to fly an F/A-18 without displays, especially if the weather is nice and you can use other nearby airplanes as a reference. That said, it's not a skill we practice much, so it's not necessarily easy either. It is definitely uncomfortable to be flying without the ability to communicate, so not having radios is perhaps more challenging and unnerving. But pulling your flight control circuit breaker . . . none of us had ever even spoken to someone who'd done that, much less done it ourselves. The jet reverts to a mode known as mech (mechanical backup), and the handling characteristics were largely unknown and, for sure, highly undesirable. That said, there was no other possible way to preserve the battery life long enough to use the flight controls when it was time to get gas. That last refuel would likely ensure Kitty would have enough gas to make it to land.

Boss gave that brief without pulling out his EPs book or any checklists. He gave the brief having spent his entire career flying that jet and understanding its systems inside and out. He gave the brief quickly and concisely because at that moment there was no telling how long Kitty would have an operating generator and time was of the essence.

There was courage in that brief. It was courage that came from experience, and it manifested itself in his confidence, which in turn gave Kitty confidence. Had Boss been less capable, professional, and experienced, it could have gone very differently. There was also courage in Kitty's response. There was no need to run through multiple other scenarios; the situation was straightforward. Our formation had gone from a happy-go-lucky group joking with each other on our radios as we ferried our jets to what would certainly be a fun week in Hawai'i to quite the opposite. No one spoke; it was totally quiet across all seven planes.

The quiet lasted for quite a long time out of respect for Kitty and his situation. It didn't seem right to continue talking or cutting up while he was sweating bullets and sucking the seat cushion up his rear considering all the unfortunate circumstances of his predicament. After what was probably about an hour of almost total silence, Kitty said, "Hey, guys, did I ever tell you about my first girlfriend?" He then regaled us with story after story for the last hour of the fight and had us all in stitches. It certainly helped that with each passing minute we were another 5–6 nm closer to land, and it became less and less likely that Kitty would end up as lunch for a hungry great white.

I don't think I could write a book about the lessons I've learned flying and serving with the finest men and women on the planet without covering courage. I simply spent too much of my career surrounded by courage to not address it; but hopefully I can do it in a way that's as unexpected as it is enlightening.

I saw some incredibly courageous acts during my twenty-five years in the Navy. I also had the pleasure of hearing stories of heroism and courage from the incredible men and women with whom I served. There certainly isn't a monopoly on courage although the term seems to be disproportionately applied to people serving in the military and other service-oriented careers, like police officers, firefighters, nurses and EMTs, and the like. That's the aspect of courage that I really want to address.

One of my favorite quotes about courage comes from none other than John Wayne, who famously said, "You don't have to fight to be brave. Millions of good, fine, decent folks show more bravery than heavyweight champs just by getting out of bed every morning, going out to do a good day's work and living the best life they know how against the law of odds."

John Wayne's quote is more on the nose than anything I could ever intelligently say or write, and I think a great majority of the most courageous acts happen routinely without anyone ever noticing. So I want to share some examples of courage that I've had the good fortune of witnessing: all very different forms of courage but all courage, nonetheless.

I'd like to start with an example that fits the traditional mold of courage that is worth retelling as many times as possible. I had the pleasure of getting to know my next-door neighbor, then-Cdr. Jeff Buschmann, while I was stationed in Pensacola, Florida. Jeff had just finished up a tour as the intelligence officer for the Naval Special Warfare Development Group (DEVGRU), also known as SEAL Team Six.

Jeff grew up in Hot Springs, Arkansas. Not only was his father a successful career naval officer, but he and Jeff had assisted a young man with a somewhat checkered past in his efforts to enlist in the Navy. That young man's name was Adam Brown, and he served our country in a manner that very few in our nation's history have. Adam had battled drug addiction prior to joining, and his battle never truly ended. Adam Brown died in a fire fight in the Kunar Province of Afghanistan on 17 March 2010. Adam's life prior to his military service and the exceptional challenges he battled while assigned to the SEAL teams (losing the use of his dominant hand and his dominant eye) were no match for the tenacity and grit of a man who didn't know the meaning of the word "quit" and whose courage was nearly without equal. Adam asked that his story be told—not the story of his victories in battle or his bravery on the field of fire but rather the story of his failures, his mistakes, and ultimately his redemption. It's truly an exceptional story, and author Eric Blehm told his story, the good and the bad, in his book *Fearless: The Undaunted Courage and Ultimate Sacrifice of Navy SEAL Team Six Operator Adam Brown.*

The book is one of the most incredible I've ever read, and it leaves you wanting to do more, to serve in a more meaningful way, to give like Adam gave. His heroism in battle was respected, if not legendary, among the most ferocious, courageous, and talented operators the world has ever known, and that's in no way hyperbole. Moreover, when Adam died in combat, he was wearing the adult-sized Batman underwear that his elementary-aged children had given him for his birthday. He told them he would wear them on each of his ops to ensure he had his superhero capabilities. Adam died a hero and will be remembered for his bravery and courage under fire, for the ever-important courage he showed in life battling his demons, and for his role as a father and husband. In that way his story tells of both kinds of courage—not just courage in battle but also courage in life, the same courage we all have within us and have the potential to imitate.

What made Adam so courageous? Is it possible to learn the skill or does it come through some other means? Is it like your height, which you cannot control in any way? Or is it closer to your weight, which you have some control over but not all are created the same? Or just maybe are we all capable of heroic levels of courage?

Let me share another story of courage, one less well known. Dr. Frank J. Weisser Jr. was born in Pittsburgh, Pennsylvania, on 9 December 1944. He lived what I think we'd all call a somewhat normal life; he went to school, focused his studies on what interested him, applied himself at work, married and had children, and did his level best to ensure his kids were better off than he was and that he gave more than he took. The exceptional parts of his life were that he earned his doctorate in nuclear particle physics in the 1960s and spent his young life working in a proton accelerator lab for Bell Labs. We'll never know the cause for certain, but likely due to the continued and daily radiation he received on the job, he was diagnosed with leukemia in the spring of 1990.

Watching my father suffer was one of the hardest things I've ever done. Watching my 6-foot, 200-pound dad wither away to almost a skeleton of a man weighing less than 120 pounds after the multiple rounds of chemo, radiation, and ultimately a bone marrow transplant was torturous for our entire family. Watching him keep his head up and face each day with positivity, energy, and a desire to not give up was the most courageous thing I've ever witnessed. "You don't have to fight to be brave" never rang truer in my mind than when watching him suffer silently, never complain, and for lack of a better term, certainly for a nuclear physicist, soldier on. Make no mistake, he was fighting; every day was a personal battle with his ever-deteriorating health and body, but it wasn't fighting as we normally think of it.

It's a different kind of courage altogether that faces a disease, a life-threatening disease. It takes courage to run into a hail of bullets, to jump on a grenade, there's no question about that. Those decisions are made in an instant and the courage is observed immediately. It's a very different kind of courage to wake up every day feeling like you wish you were dead, having very little or possibly even no hope of a recovery, yet still finding the will and the energy to live and to go on. My father's courage was unmatched in my mind, and I didn't understand where he found the drive and the ability until I had children of my own. There's a deep desire in us all to protect and defend. As fathers its incumbent upon us to give our children everything we have for their benefit and for the good of our civilization.

For eleven years my father lived a completely selfless existence. He couldn't do anything physically demanding, even walking across the room required supplemental oxygen, so hobbies were out. He could barely eat anything after the cancer destroyed his throat, making tiny morsels of food get stuck, unable to be swallowed. All the little things we each live for were taken from him; but he had his family and he had his work, and he took great pride in both.

My father died on 19 June 2001 after a long, hard, and courageous battle with leukemia. He left us too soon; there's no question about that. He left a daughter in college, a son in flight school, and a widow who'd devoted the past eleven years of her life to his 24/7 care and well-being. He also left us with a near–picture perfect example of what marathon courage looks like. He left us with the memory and the example of a man who understood the meaning of selflessness. In the same way a Medal of Honor recipient who dives on a grenade to save his fellow men inspires us, so too does this type of courage.

No one awards medals to men and women who show that kind of courage and bravery, but it's there, nonetheless. That particular courage fits the definition to a T. I used to think that if you looked up the word "courage" in the dictionary, you'd see his face.

While we're on the subject of a father's courage, I'd like to share another example that ties both types together. A close friend of mine, Patrick O'Mara, graduated the Naval Academy a year before I did, in 1999. He went through flight school to be a Navy pilot, and he also became a career F/A-18 pilot. We served together as department heads in Strike Fighter Squadron 97 (VFA-97) and deployed together in 2011–12 on board the USS *John C. Stennis.* Prior to that time, Pat went through TOPGUN and was an instructor at the Navy's Weapons School at NAS Lemoore in California and ultimately had command of VFA-97 a few years later.

Pat also has the distinction of being what I called the First Blue Angel Baby because both his mother and father were Blue Angels. His father, Kevin O'Mara, was a Marine captain and served as Blue Angel #2, the Right Wingman, in 1970–71 when they flew the F-4 Phantom. His mother, Mary Russell, was the first female officer on the Blue Angels, having joined in 1968 and served as their public affairs officer. The two were married a few years later, and my friend Pat and his older sister Katie became the First Blue Angel Babies.

Pat had a lot to live up to, and he knew it. I can't imagine it's easy being the child of a Marine fighter pilot who was both a Blue Angel and a commanding officer of a Marine fighter squadron, not to mention having a mother who was the first female Blue Angels officer. Pat, though, made them both very proud and had an exceptional career. Pat followed in his father's footsteps and married a military officer, a flight surgeon and ultimately an ophthalmologist. As you might expect, military families and the constant deployments are never easy to manage, but even more so when one spouse is a successful and busy physician. Pat's hard work and success throughout his career made him an obvious choice for promotion to captain and subsequent follow-on command tours as a captain. This career path often leads down the road to promotion to admiral and serving in some incredibly important positions.

From my own experience and witnessing my friends and colleagues find themselves in similar positions, the drive to push ahead careerwise is quite tempting. After competing and excelling, eventually being selected for larger and more prestigious commands is the affirmation and the reward for hard work and success. This same sentiment and drive are prevalent throughout all businesses; the military isn't alone in having motivated and career-oriented folks working their way up the chain. Very few can resist that urge and willingly give up on their chosen path for other reasons, for selfless reasons. Pat did just that despite being in a position where his upward trajectory was essentially limitless.

When we talk about Navy pilots, to be successful they're evaluated in three categories: Good Pilot, Good Officer, and Good Person. The pilot part is fairly straightforward. The Good Officer part basically means they excel in all other aspects of the job outside of the jet, which are numerous and certainly ever more important as they get more senior. The final category, Good Person, speaks to the fact that other people want to be around them, at work, on liberty, wherever. It's the person who looks out for you, cares for you, and will have your back when you need it. If someone has two of the three, they'll succeed in the business, but if they have all three they'll excel—no question. Pat had all three and in spades; he was destined for the Navy's top tiers of leadership. That said, he recognized that he couldn't support his wife in her career the way he wanted to and he couldn't be as present as he wanted to be for his son if he continued along in his career as a Navy pilot. With each successive promotion and with each successive command, your job gets busier and more stressful and your time to yourself gets less and less. I have a great deal of respect for my friends who have continued on the path, and I'm grateful they're willing and able to serve our country in such a meaningful way.

I also have a great deal of respect for the guys like Pat who are willing to be courageous and make an incredibly hard decision. It's certainly not as simple as just announcing you're done; the process of getting out and retiring at that point in a career will certainly be met with many senior officers and mentors doing their level best to convince you to stay in. They'll make pleas; they'll restate how important you are to the safety and survival of our country. It's very hard to say no, especially for someone who has always worked to, if not been institutionalized to, sacrifice for a higher calling. Making that decision takes courage and a great deal of it; and once again, it's the kind of courage that isn't recognized, and sometimes it's even disparaged. I'm proud of Pat for making an incredibly hard, courageous decision, and I'm quite sure his family is even more grateful and will certainly benefit the most from that sort of selfless courage. I firmly believe that one day his son will reflect and realize that his dad gave up his personal, and maybe even prideful, desires to promote and excel in the military because he placed more value in being present for his family. He made being a husband and father his priority, and that's no easy thing to do.

The military in no way has cornered the market on principled family decisions that take courage; quite the opposite, I'm sure. I highlight Pat's decision to illustrate the situation and the value behind making a selfless decision. We each have so many of these opportunities, and all the people I know who have made them find that the satisfaction far outweighs any possible regret.

There's another kind of courage tied to our careers that isn't necessarily the courage to walk away. It's the courage to do the job the way you believe it should be done rather than the way you think will most likely lead to your success. It's the sort of courage that requires being willing to lose your job or lose your future opportunities because you believe so strongly in your cause. I will share how this works in naval aviation knowing full well that all companies, big and small, operate in a very similar fashion, and this type of courage translates across many civilian situations.

The military is a pyramid when it comes to promotions and command opportunities. To put it into perspective, a typical single-seat F/A-18 squadron has fifteen to eighteen pilots. Nine to twelve of them are junior officers flying in their first squadron, and they're typically there for three years. Three to four of them are department heads, essentially mid-level officers having flown for the past ten years or more. The two most senior officers are the executive officer (XO—our second in command) and our commanding officer, the skipper.

So the numbers aren't terribly tricky or confusing. Of the nine to twelve pilots who start out in a squadron, only a third of them will be chosen to be department heads, and of those, only half of them will be chosen to be in command of their own squadron. Each aircraft carrier has eight squadrons: fighters, jammers, controllers, and helicopters. Above the squadron commanding officers sits the commander of the air group (CAG), who is responsible for all the squadrons and their aircraft and personnel, and the CAG's onboard peer is the commanding officer of the aircraft carrier, who is responsible for the ship and its respective crew. Above them is only the admiral, who commands the entire strike group, which is made up of multiple ships and submarines. To move upward, you get the idea, you must excel ahead of your peers to be selected for subsequent promotions and commands. The Navy distills it down simply to, Sustained Superior Performance at Sea.

It was certainly my experience that the officers who most desired to move up often acted in a way to please their respective bosses. I also strongly believe it's imperative that our commanding officers execute their duties and responsibilities in such ways as the boss expects and has directed. Sometimes though, that concept can come into conflict with the autonomy of leadership.

Leadership works most effectively when it's autonomous to a high degree, meaning a leader can operate with little to no intervention. If a CAG allows the squadron commanding officers to have the autonomy to make decisions, then they can best and most accurately determine who the finest leaders are. Although nearly everyone knows and understands that concept in theory, very few on either side of that relationship seem to adhere to it in practice. What happens all too often is that the CAG wants to succeed and be selected for flag rank and various admiral commands, so it's imperative that his commanding officers are successful to ensure the entire air wing is successful. The CAG held those officers' job years before and apparently did it well enough to move up the pyramid. So the CAG is quite convinced his way is the right way and is also very likely to share those lessons, ostensibly through mentorship, to those under his charge.

What, then, do the commanding officers do? Do they take the CAG's input, advice, and recommendations and follow them as gospel? Do they take a portion and use it when it works the best and makes the most sense? Do they disregard it entirely and go about it their own way, the way they believe will be most effective? Any of those avenues are perfectly fine solutions, and they'll only know if they chose correctly when they have their performance review and find out how they were ranked relative to their peers.

I had the pleasure to serve with another incredible naval officer and pilot, Cdr. Matthew "TOD" Doyle. TOD, like Pat, was also the son of a naval aviator and had an incredible example to follow and emulate. As a group, most Navy pilots are very similar. We're similar in how we interact, how we lead, and how we respond to our leaders. TOD was different, certainly a standard deviation or two away from the norm, and I loved that about him. He wasn't just different; he was absolutely fearless when it came to his future. Make no mistake, TOD wanted to excel in the military and in naval aviation, of that there was no question. TOD just intended to do it his way, and that meant being an expert at basically everything.

To say he knew our airplane inside and out would be an understatement. He was a test pilot who'd graduated from the Navy's yearlong Test Pilot School at NAS Patuxent

River, Maryland. That school blends flying with intense academics to ensure its graduates understand all aspects of aviation at a postgraduate level. TOD also understood maintenance, which *very* few pilots do. He read our maintenance bible, the OPNAV 4790, cover to cover and could almost recite it chapter and verse. This frustrated some in our maintenance department to no end since they were used to dealing with pilots who really had no clue what they did and how they were supposed to do it. TOD also made himself an expert in the other squadron functions of administration and safety. In short, he was a force to be reckoned with.

When we were serving together as department heads, we were led by a commanding officer who was nearly the exact opposite of TOD in almost every way. Rather than being quiet and reflective, he was short tempered and impulsive. Rather than being a recognized expert, he was effectively the opposite. Having a skipper like this was a problem for all of us, but it was more of a problem for TOD because he couldn't quite process the overall ineptitude; it was completely anathema to him. One "fun" night sticks out in my memory that ties back into a story I relayed in chapter 3 (the chapter on trust). That was the night I landed, with Nemo's help, in a jet experiencing an electrical failure. Following that landing, what should have been viewed as a successful recovery of a jet during a challenging emergency somehow took a different turn. Our deputy air wing commander (DCAG) was confused when he saw the airplane flying in formation break away rather than the lead aircraft. As I explained previously, this was my request made from total trust and confidence in Nemo to back me up. Nonetheless, our DCAG viewed it as nonstandard and was upset about it. The fact that he was upset about it didn't bother me very much because, as it turned out, DCAG wasn't a pilot. He was a naval flight officer who sat in the back seat and as such had never flown an airplane. He was still senior to us and our deputy commander, so for that he got his due respect; but I didn't think it was his place to tell me how to fly my single-seat airplane.

One person who very much did intend to listen to DCAG was our skipper. He was more than happy to take DCAG's feedback and then make sweeping changes to how we operated as a squadron, and only after dressing down our whole squadron during a meeting in our ready room. The "fun" didn't end there, though. After the ready room meeting, our skipper took the four of us department heads into his stateroom for yet another discussion. It should be worth nothing that staterooms on aircraft carriers are not very large—every inch of space is used as is typical on boats. Moreover, it's a special privilege of the senior officers and commanders to have their own private room. Even their own private room was small, however. It had a small closet for uniforms, a small desk to work at, and then along the far wall was a couch to be used for meetings just like this, but that couch space also doubled as bed space. The couch would fold into the wall, revealing a bed slightly smaller than a normal twin bed.

On this particular evening, the four of us were "welcomed" into his stateroom, and we sat down like children ready for our punishment. We sat on the couch, squeezing tightly together with our hands and arms more like schoolchildren, left hand–left knee, right hand–right knee style. We were then reprimanded for how we handled the emergency situation and told repeatedly that we'd let down our skipper and DCAG. We sat there like good little boys (naval officers) and took our licking, ready to move on and be off the couch. When it was finally over, the skipper said something to the effect of, "Anything to add?" We all shook our heads no, ready to leave. Well, all of us except TOD. Frustrated at having had to sit there and listen to someone who couldn't carry his water pail in any sense, TOD proceeded to challenge our skipper, albeit respectfully, and go item by item refuting and correcting him on everything wrong he had just said. He also added, as a bonus, that the three of us involved in this emergency recovery had over 8,000 hours of experience flying F/A-18s while the DCAG had exactly 0 hours. TOD turned the whole situation on its head, and the room basically erupted. Our short time on the couch turned out to be much longer, and it would have been considerably worse had it not been so enjoyable to watch TOD surgically dismantle the skipper with each of his comments.

Needless to say, the event didn't end well, despite us eventually being told to leave. Yet I left with a great deal of respect for TOD. Most of us had learned to bite our tongue when we saw things we disagreed with because it's not generally acceptable to argue with the skipper. That wasn't a consideration for TOD; he had a kind of courage I didn't fully understand or appreciate. He was far less worried about how he would be ranked or evaluated than he was concerned about ensuring he spoke his mind and making sure his voice and his perspective were heard. As it turns out, he was exactly right, and it took him showing that courage for us as a squadron to find our way through this situation.

Rarely in my military career did I see individuals speak up to, much less correct, their immediate supervisor or their skipper. Having the courage to do it was and is a rare thing, but the benefits of doing so are too numerous to name. None of us are infallible, but sometimes the power hierarchy prevents those in charge from receiving feedback. It takes having courage to announce to the emperor that he is wearing no clothes.

At one point during our deployment, some in our squadron were remarking that we hadn't seen much of our CAG. Rather than splitting his time equally among the squadrons, he primarily had been flying and socializing with the two Super Hornet squadrons, and as such he likely didn't have a good sense of how we were doing. The rest of us sat around and complained about it, but as I said, TOD was different. TOD, during a check-out brief before heading home from deployment, found the respectful way to let him know that our squadron felt like he was an absent leader. Different leaders would handle feedback like that from a junior officer very differently, and some might consider trying to fire the person on the spot. That wasn't the case, and instead the CAG came down to our ready room that afternoon, just to visit. He came by a lot more after that as well. That speaks volumes for a variety of reasons. TOD had the courage to do what he thought was right and chose to speak up, and he did so in a respectful way. Also, and maybe even more important, our CAG had the courage to take constructive criticism from someone much junior to him. That's a whole different and critical kind of courage and one that great teams are built on.

As I said before in the chapter on communication (chapter 4), it takes courage to give constructive criticism, just as TOD did. It's also a skill and a challenge and takes courage to receive it, especially to receive it with grace. It takes remembering, in that moment, that it wasn't easy for the individual providing this criticism to give it in the first place. They're likely nervous and uncomfortable, far more so than even you are as the one being criticized or corrected. Being able to understand that, to process that, and to appreciate their perspective sets apart good leaders and managers from the great ones. Imagine in the moment you're being criticized or corrected stepping away from the natural pain and frustration that exists in that moment. Imagine if you could process, in that moment, the other individual's perspective. If you have the mental clarity and strength and presence of mind to do that, your reaction will be considerably more appropriate and professional. If it were easy to do, we'd all react this way. It's not, though; it takes courage.

One final type of courage I want to address is the courage to own your mistakes and, maybe even more powerfully, own the mistakes of others. This might be the rarest of all types of courage, which is why I saved it for last. In the communication chapter I covered the idea of being your own harshest critic and why it's so critical to the communications of a high-functioning team. What I left off in that chapter is how it's accomplished and why it's so rare. It's because so few of us have the courage to do it.

What does it mean to "own your mistake," and why is it so hard to do? When you own your mistake you're taking responsibility for what you did wrong, sure, but you're also in a way diminishing yourself, or at least it might feel that way. As I explained earlier, doing so makes you vulnerable, and most of us shy away, or totally steer clear, from that state of being. If you can, though, for a brief moment appreciate the perspective of those around you rather than how you feel as you own your mistake; imagine being on the other end of the interaction. Remember a time when a coworker or friend took responsibility for something they did wrong. Did you think less of them? Did you trust them less because they admitted they made a mistake?

The answer, of course, is no.

Despite how it feels to own your mistake, despite how it feels to make yourself vulnerable, the result is always the opposite for those around you. They end up respecting you more, trusting you more, and wanting to have the courage to act the same. Your courage to some degree allows them to.

On a beautiful summer morning in early July of 2008, I strapped into the front seat of an F/A-18B, BUNO 161943. I was joined by my other Crew Chief for the #7 jet, Aviation Structural Mechanic (Safety Equipment) Petty Officer 2nd Class (AME2) Austin Armstrong. Austin was in his first year as the Crew Chief for the #7 jet and was learning the ropes from my aforementioned Crew Chief, Deo. Austin had an incredible amount of energy for the job, he exuded positivity at every turn, and he made being at work fun for everyone around him. He also was giving 110 percent to learn from Deo and be the best possible "7 Geek." As I mentioned briefly before, the job of the 7 Crew Chief is a highly sought-after job on the Blue Angels as the chosen individual gets to fly every single week to each air show and moreover spends a great deal of time briefing and preparing a wide range of celebrities for backseat rides.

Ever since I had been chosen the fall prior when I joined the Blue Angels to be the #7 pilot, I had been paired up with Austin. He was in his second year on the Blue Angels but first as the 7 Crew Chief, so we both went through a few months together of training in the fall of 2007. We spent part of the 2007 air show season with that year's #7 pilot, Nate Miller, flying with Deo in his back seat while I would fly with Austin to each show. Once we arrived, we would mirror our mentors each day and learn as quickly as we could what was required of the new job. As such, Austin and I became close quickly and developed a very special bond that most Naval Officers and Sailors never attain. We spent hours together in the jet, setting up the air shows, briefing the FAA, air show staffs, local police, etc. . . . to ensure our show went off smoothly. We shared meals each week, we spoke dozens of times each day, all very abnormal for the traditional Navy relationships between Officers and Enlisted, but then again, the Blue Angels weren't your typical command and the relationship between the pilots and their crew chiefs was even more atypical, in a very special way.

So Austin and I manned up for our flight together that morning heading to Traverse City, Michigan for their annual National Cherry Festival Air Show. The flight from Pensacola to Traverse City was just under 900 nm and as such was a touch too far for our two-seat F/A-18B, so we planned the most efficient fuel stop we could manage, which was almost exactly halfway there at Scott AFB just southeast of St. Louis. We took off the minute our control tower in Pensacola opened and made great time getting to

Scott. The weather both in St. Louis and Traverse City was beautiful, and everything was lining up to be a great day. When we landed, we taxied to the refueling area and shut down. We had previously coordinated for a "quick turn" which meant we requested a fuel truck be standing by and we would get gas and takeoff as quickly as possible. Our Standard Operating Procedure (SOP) at the time was for the 7 Crew Chief to get out of the jet, conduct a postflight inspection, oversee the refueling process, which was done by a local base employee, then preflight the jet and climb back in. Meanwhile, as the #7 pilot, I wouldn't even unstrap. I would pull out my cell phone, call for an updated weather brief, update the air show staff on my ETA and call back to my immediate supervisor at the Blue Angels, our Operations Officer and #5 pilot, to update him on my status. This process usually worked extremely efficiently and effectively, and that morning was no different.

After Austin had strapped back in, we were off. We taxied to the runway, ran up our engines, and immediately added full power as we roared off down the runway for our short flight to Traverse City. The jet flew a bit like a rocket ship, as it always seemed to in the early morning hours when the temperatures were cooler. We got the gear and flaps up, were cleared on course, and I immediately pulled back on the stick to an accelerated climbing left-hand turn towards Michigan. It was just after I got the nose heading north that the whole jet felt like it exploded. The noise was deafening, the jet shook violently, and it felt like every warning and caution light went off simultaneously as the jet rapidly lost its thrust. As I mentioned previously while discussing how Navy pilots are taught to deal with adversity, this time was no different. The best way to proceed is to take a deep breath (sit on your hands) and then process what had happened. It became clear that we'd lost our right engine which was indicating high temperatures and no thrust. Unfortunately, the right engine also powers our right hydraulic system which in turn powers our brakes and steering. If everything had been straightforward and we'd known exactly what had caused it, we could have circled overhead, burned down some of the fuel to lower our landing weight, and arranged to have arresting gear raised in order to take a short field arrestment and therefore reduce issues that could arise from having no brakes or steering. As it was though, we had no idea why the engine had exploded unexpectedly. We hadn't seen any birds, and we hadn't had trouble or indications of problems on the previous flight. As such, I was in the mood to get on deck reasonably fast lest something similar happen to the other engine, and so I turned downwind, declared an emergency, and told the tower I was landing on the same runway I had just departed from moments ago. The runway was 10,000 feet long, so plenty long enough to land and roll to a stop without brakes, and I decided in that moment that it was our best option. We landed uneventfully in less than a minute and rolled out without the use of brakes and used our emergency brake power to use differential steering to clear the runway. Once we were stopped safely on the taxiway, I raised the canopy and began to unstrap in an effort to figure out what had gone wrong.

It wasn't immediately obvious to me what had happened when I heard Austin's voice from the ground below. I looked down on the right side of the jet and he was standing there on the ground and looking up at me. Even fifteen years later, I'm not sure how he was able to unstrap so fast, not even use the ladder which hadn't been deployed, walk back along the narrow fuselage, slide off the wing, and deduce immediately what had gone wrong, but that's exactly what he had done. As he looked up at me, I can remember it like it was yesterday, he said, "Sir, I screwed up."

How Austin handled himself in that moment and in the weeks and months to come was, in my mind, the definition of courage. Here he was, a somewhat new Crew Chief in a position with a great deal of responsibility. He was fairly young, early twenties, and it would have been reasonable, if not expected, for him to try and make excuses or place the blame elsewhere, but that's not what he did at all. He owned his mistake from the moment it happened and never once shied away from the responsibility in the months to come.

When he slid off the front of the wing, he immediately saw that the refueling panel on the forward right side of the airplane hadn't been closed and secured properly and the fuel cap, a heavy metal cap, had been left dangling by a thin chain. As the speed increased on takeoff, the chain had snapped under the force of the acceleration and the cap had unluckily gone right into the right engine air intake and caused the engine to explode. It was Austin's job to preflight the airplane and he'd missed a single step, something he'd done correctly hundreds of times before. Moreover, having refueled hundreds, if not thousands, of times over my career, never once had I seen the refueling personnel not replace the cap and close the refueling panel door.

The critical part to me was that Austin could have tried to say that he did check it and verified that it was on and the refueling door was closed. No one could have proved him wrong. I suspect that a lot of people, maybe even most folks, would have probably done just that, certainly in that initial moment. It's always in the initial moment that our character is really tested and how we react is most revealing of who we really are. Austin was an extremely bright young man and could have fabricated a very believable story and likely nothing would have happened to him. In fact, Austin could have easily blamed the man that refueled us, whose job it was to put the fuel cap back on, but he didn't, never once.

From the moment he slid off the ladder, Austin owned his mistake, he owned the mistake of our refueler, and most importantly to me, he owned my mistake as the Pilot in Command. Ultimately the Navy allows us an incredible degree of leadership autonomy, in many disparate ways, but what it requires from us in return is an equally incredible degree of responsibility. In this case, as the pilot who signed for that jet, it was my responsibility, and the mistake was mine.

Austin was wrecked by what happened, and worse, he knew what would happen to him as a result. He would lose his qualifications, his ability to work on and maintain our jets, what he'd spent the past two years working towards. He'd be put on a sort of maintenance probation until he could prove to his maintenance leadership that he'd learned his lesson and wouldn't make that sort of mistake again. Worse still, he would be temporarily removed from his position as the #7 Crew Chief and not allowed to travel to the air shows. He knew all of that in the instant he saw the fuel cap, but it didn't change for a minute his first words of "Sir, I screwed up."

What's more exceptional still is that because of him losing his quals and because of him being taken off the road from participating in air shows, it became more of a marathon of courage. And as I described previously, this is far more challenging and taxing than momentary courage, which he certainly displayed as well. The lesson he taught the rest of the Blue Angel team in those weeks and months that followed was that he understood the meaning of courage and he believed that he had it in him to make a Nice Correction. He knew, even at a very young age, that his character mattered more than his qualifications. Somehow, he intuitively knew that if he suffered the repercussions of his mistake with confidence and humbleness, he'd be better off for having made the mistake.

That takes courage. It takes courage to admit when you're wrong, and it takes even more courage to own this mistake of others as well. It takes an enormous amount of courage to do all that and to do it with your head held high. Austin did just that. Despite his embarrassment and frustration, he kept his head held high, he remained the positive person who had motivated all his fellow Sailors and Marines before the mishap and continued to do so after the mishap.

The most impactful part of this all to me was that as I'd mentioned, it was ultimately my fault, my failure. Furthermore, I didn't handle it nearly as well. I was noticeably frustrated by what had happened and by how it was subsequently handled. It was then, that as a senior Lieutenant, I was able to take a lesson from a junior Sailor. It wasn't the first time I learned a valuable lesson from someone junior to me and it wasn't the last, but it was one of most memorable to me because of the courage Austin displayed. It's a lesson worth repeating for all of us who are in positions of leadership that we can often learn more from those working for us than we can from those we're working for. Having incredible Sailors like Austin to learn from was one of the many blessings of my military career.

On a very positive Blue Angel note, our team allows for mistakes and for Nice Corrections. Austin did earn back his quals, and quickly, and was able to resume his duties as the #7 Crew Chief as the season progressed. Also, on that particular day, in a near-perfect illustration of the incredible teamwork of the Blue Angels, I called the Operations Officer and explained what had happened minutes after we landed. He informed our Boss and our C-130 crew who mobilized instantly and landed in Scott AFB barely an hour later. As the ramp of the C-130 came down, a team of the Navy's best maintainers poured out of the Hercules and did what normally takes a squadron a full day in a matter of what seemed like minutes. They removed the damaged motor and replaced it with a known-good motor, meaning no maintenance test flight was required. Austin and I were off to Traverse City and landed there in time for lunch. That weekend's show went off without a hitch, and what could have been a catastrophic mistake caused only a few hours' delay because of the exceptional professionals who were our Blue Angels team.

I witnessed many courageous things during my time flying Navy jets off aircraft carriers. I remember many nights when my fellow squadron mates or pilots in our various air wings were flying missions and encountered a variety of malfunctions that put them and their aircraft in extremis and in the dark of night. There's an expression of aviation that it is always better to be on the ground wishing you were flying than flying and wishing you were on the ground. I've been continually impressed by the courage, bravery, and calmness of my fellow aviators as they deal with incredibly challenging scenarios in harsh and unforgiving environments and still handle it with poise and bravery. I also saw some of those same people make equally courageous decisions that didn't involve flying at all.

Perhaps Winston Churchill said it best when he remarked, "Fear is a reaction. Courage is a decision." We are each given opportunities every day to make courageous decisions, to "do the right thing." How we choose to react and act are in large part driven by the examples of courage we've seen and experienced throughout our lives. Hopefully my shared experiences can in a small way illustrate the many forms courage can take in our everyday lives. I for one believe we can all benefit from the examples provided to us, both by those fighting and by those showing bravery in a variety of other ways.

ACKNOWLEDGMENTS

I WOULD LIKE TO REITERATE what I said in the opening of this book, not to repeat myself but rather to reinforce the most critical aspect: this book is my small attempt to recognize some exceptional men and women and to tell of their legacies and impacts on our country.

Serving our country for so many years has been a journey and an incredibly exciting one at that. The same is true about collecting these stories and recounting them with my friends and mentors—the journey has continued and I'm profoundly grateful for the opportunity and humbled that some might be interested, even inspired by them.

I've tried my best to convey the most impactful lessons I learned during my time flying for the U.S. Navy. The vehicle for these lessons was the F/A-18, and hopefully this book is as successful in illustrating them as the jet has been in patrolling and protecting our skies over the last forty years of its service. Having been retired for just over three years as I write this, I feel strongly that these lessons are applicable as much in everyday life, regardless of your profession, as they are when flying off aircraft carriers and in air shows. If I had one regret to share, it would just be that I didn't recognize at the time, and in the moment, just what exceptional people I was fortunate to work and fly with. That's only truly become apparent to me in my military retirement as I search for the same sort of meaning and passion, trying to surround myself with the same kind of men and women who are both genuine and exceptional in all they do.

I would like to take a moment to recognize those who have influenced this journey:

Capt. and Mrs. Sandy Coward IV—USNA sponsor family

Brian Fairweather (USN) and Holly Fryburger (USMC)—USNA friends and confidants

Brad Davis—primary flight training instructor and "Onwing"

Dave Silkey and Frank Morley—VFA commanding officers and mentors

Blue Angels crew chiefs—Deo Harrypersaud, Austin Armstrong, Alicia Raper, Cory Keller, Anthony Koppi, Justin Hanks, Rich Sweeney, and Aldriick Kittles

VFA HOPA—Matt Doyle, Pat O'Mara, Tom Hoyt, Chris Miranda, and unquestionably our best example of consistent and principled leadership throughout many trying times, Scott "Spill" Smith

Scott Butler, Tim Kinsella, and Scott Janik—my leaders, my mentors, and my friends

Brian Ferguson and Kevin Larosa—*Top Gun: Maverick* liaison and aerial coordinator

Blue Angels sailors and Marines—the most inspiring and impressive team I have ever witnessed, and I am honored to have served with them

Blue Angels officers—to the men and women I was privileged to share *high trust* with from 2008 until 2021. They are the most incredible people I have met to date, and the barometer to whom I compare all others, though I suspect I'll never find their equals.

Steve Catalano—my Naval Institute Press editor without whose vision and direction none of this would have happened. Somehow Steve knew better than I how to tell the stories and was able to instantly recognize the most gripping and impactful portions to best illustrate the material. Any possible success this book might have is because of him.

My mother- and father-in-law, Don and Joan Plunkett, have been the most incredibly supportive in-laws a man could ask for and have freely given of themselves to ensure our family's success. My mother, Phyllis Weisser, was the embodiment of selfless in all she did for both her husband and her children, and she provided me a near-perfect example of sacrifice and strength.

My three children, Kendall, Ben, and Caroline, didn't ask to serve their country, but the service was imparted on them nonetheless. That's true of all military children. Without their strength, resilience, and love, our family could not have served in the manner we did. No matter what I accomplish in my life, nothing will ever come close to equaling even a small fraction of how proud I am of each of them.

At the most basic level, none of this would have been possible without my wife of twenty years, Bethany Plunkett Weisser, being both my foundation and my exclamation point. My words will fall short, so I'll say simply that she proudly accepted the task of being a wife and a mother to a husband who spent many years away, and she bore the burden with grace throughout. Our children are unquestionably our crowning achievement, and they are exceptional because of her.

> ***"Once you have tasted flight, you will forever walk the earth with your eyes turned SKYWARD, for there you have been, and there you will always long to return."***
>
> ***—JOHN SECONDARI***

ABOUT THE AUTHOR

CDR. FRANK WEISSER, USN (RET.), is a two-time Blue Angels pilot who was deployed in combat three separate times, including to Afghanistan and Iraq. He has accumulated more than 5,000 flight hours in military jets and nearly 500 carrier arrested landings. He earned a master's degree in systems analysis from the Naval Postgraduate School in September 2009. His decorations include multiple Meritorious Service medals, Strike Flight Air medals, and various personal and unit awards. Because of his experience flying both at extreme low altitudes and inverted, he piloted many of the most complex and memorable air combat scenes for *Top Gun: Maverick*. He can be found at his website, www.frankweisser.net, and can be contacted via email at frank@frankweisser.net.